Changing
Lenses

Changing Lenses

Howard Zehr

A Christian Peace Shelf Selection

HERALD PRESS
Scottdale, Pennsylvania
Waterloo, Ontario

Library of Congress Cataloging-in-Publication Data
Zehr, Howard.
      Changing lenses : a new focus for crime and
justice / Howard J.
  Zehr.
            p. cm. — (A Christian peace shelf selection)
      Includes bibliographical references.
      ISBN 0-8361-3512-1 :
      1. Criminal justice, Administration of.   2. Punishment.
  3. Reconciliation.   4. Victims of
crimes.   5. Criminals.   I. Title.
  II. Series.
  K5001.Z43   1990
  364.6—dc20   89-77873

The paper used in this publication is recycled and meets the minimum requirements of American National Standard for Information Sciences—Permanence of Paper for Printed Library Materials, ANSI Z39.48-1984.

CHANGING LENSES
Copyright © 1990 by Herald Press, Scottdale, Pa. 15683
    Published simultaneously in Canada by Herald Press,
    Waterloo, Ont. N2L 6H7. All rights reserved
Library of Congress Catalog Card Number: 89-77873
International Standard Book Number: 0-8361-3512-2
Printed in the United States of America
Design by Paula M. Johnson
Cover photographs by Howard Zehr

2 3 4 5 6 7 8 9 9 96 95 94 93

Psalm 103

Yahweh is tender and compassionate,
slow to anger, most loving;
his indignation does not last for ever,
his resentment exists a short time only;
he never treats us, never punishes us,
as our guilt and our sins deserve.

—Jerusalem Bible, vv. 8-10

Contents

Preface

This book has emerged from experience, reading, and discussions over a number of years. It is a work of synthesis more than invention. Consequently, it draws on the ideas and experiences of many. I owe appreciation to numerous people, more than I can possibly acknowledge, but at least I want to express my appreciation. . . .

To my Canadian colleague Dave Worth who has encouraged and cajoled me to finish this book, and also has provided many ideas and suggestions.

To Martin Wright, Millard Lind, Alan Kreider, and W. H. Allchin who read the manuscript, encouraged me to go on, and made many helpful suggestions.

To those whose contributions ·I have tried to acknowledge in this book. To the many who have made a contribution in ways I am not able to cite specifically. And especially to Nils Christie and Herman Bianchi whose writings and discussions have helped to point a way.

To the participants in conferences and seminars in the United States, Canada, and England who have listened to and tested these ideas over the past few years.

To the hundreds of people involved in the VORP movement—in the United States, Canada, England, and elsewhere—whose determination and examples have given me courage and a grounding in real life.

To Mennonite Central Committee U.S. which has given me encouragement and space to develop my ideas and write them down. H. A. Penner, former director of MCC U.S. Program, in particular encouraged me to carry on.

To John Harding and the Hampshire Probation Service, who invited me to England, made me feel welcome, and gave me a home for working on this manuscript while there.

To Doris Rupe, who provided me with a quiet place to write away from my office.

Many have helped to shape this work. Nevertheless, in the end I take responsibility for the contents, which do not necessarily reflect the position of Mennonite Central Committee nor of those who I have named above.

—*Howard Zehr*

PART I

The Experience of Crime

CHAPTER 1

A Vignette

This book is about principles and ideals. It seeks—
perhaps presumptuously—to identify and evaluate
some of the basic assumptions we make about crime,
about justice, about how we live together. It attempts
to outline briefly how we came to have these assumptions and to suggest some alternatives.

Such an effort involves abstractions, but it cannot be
limited to them. We must begin by entering into the
actual experience of crime and of justice as deeply as
we can. Only with a firm footing in such reality can we
begin to understand what we do, why we do it, and—
hopefully—what we might do differently.

But an understanding of the experience of crime is
not an easy undertaking, and it is not one that most of
us approach willingly. To confront what it means to
victimize or to be victimized by another person sparks
intense emotions which are often frightening and
which we would rather let lie. Unless we have experienced crime directly, we may find it difficult to
empathize fully. Nevertheless, we must try, realizing
that the attempt will be incomplete and perhaps painful.

This book, then, begins at that point.

The Story

Several years ago I sat with a seventeen-year-old defendant in a courtroom in a small American town. A
colleague and I had been asked to prepare a sentencing
proposal to submit to the court. We were now there,
awaiting sentencing by the judge.

The events leading up to this point make a sorry
story. This young man (he was then 16) had used a
knife to confront a young woman in a dark hallway. In
the ensuing scuffle she lost an eye. Now his fate was to
be decided.

Although details are uncertain, something like this
seems to have unfolded. The young man, who came
from an unhappy—probably abusive—home situation
had decided to run away with his girl friend, but
lacked the necessary money. He had no record of
violence. But television apparently convinced him that
if he threatened someone, they would hand over their
money and his problem would be solved.

In choosing a victim, he picked a young woman he
sometimes saw around town. On several occasions he
had attempted to talk with her but had been rebuffed.
Since he assumed her to be well off, she seemed a
logical choice.

So he waited in the hallway of her apartment with a
knife in his hand, his face masked. (He claims he had
deliberately picked a small knife.) When she entered,
he grabbed her from behind. But instead of passively
handing over her money as he expected, the young
woman panicked—as most of us would—and began to
scream and struggle. The young man's mother later
mentioned that he never could stand to have voices
raised against him, that he tended to get irrational
when that happened. Perhaps this explains his behavior, then, because when she struggled, he too panicked,
stabbing her a number of times, including in the eye.

They entered her apartment. Here their stories differ as to whether he held her captive or was attempting to help. He claims that he was taking her for help and that she was cooperating. At the time of arrest he was reported to have said, "I didn't mean it, I didn't mean it. I didn't want to hurt nobody. Tell her I'm sorry." At any rate, he was arrested as they were leaving the apartment. Eventually he was convicted and now was awaiting sentence.

In the tiny courtroom in this small community he sat with his attorney at a table facing the judge. Behind him sat his family. In the back row sat the family and relatives of the victim. Scattered through the room were a few interested onlookers and criminal justice professionals.

Before he was sentenced I presented my sentencing proposal which called for a limited prison term, supervision, restitution to the victim, restitution to the community, counseling, education, structured living, and employment. He was asked whether he had anything to say.

He talked about his sorrow for what he had done, of his attempt to understand what it meant for the young woman. "I realize," he said, "I have caused a lot of pain. Miss _____ lost something she will never get back. I would gladly give her my eye to see through. I am sorry for what I have done, and I ask that I be forgiven. I don't wish to cause [her] family any harm in later years, no matter how long it will be." Then came time for sentencing.

Before pronouncing sentence, however, the judge methodically enumerated the usual goals of sentences: the need for retribution, the need to isolate offenders from society, the need to rehabilitate, the need to deter. He noted the need for offenders to be held accountable for their actions.

The judge also discussed this young man's intent in committing the crime. He had been charged with armed robbery and assault with intent to kill. The judge appeared to agree with the offender's version that he did not intend to kill when he undertook the robbery. However, it was the judge's inference that he had formed the intent during the course of the struggle and thus that the charge was both accurate and serious.

Then he pronounced sentence. The young man was given a sentence of 20-85 years in prison with no possibility of parole or good time before the minimum was served. He would be at least 37 when he emerged. "I trust," the judge admonished this youth as he pronounced this sentence, "that there you will forget the patterns of behavior which led to this violent offense."

That this story is a tragedy can hardly be denied. It is, however, a tragedy which was soon abstracted into a different kind of drama. Instead of a tragic confrontation between two individuals, the legal process and the media transformed it into a *crime* involving a *criminal* and—it is only secondarily remembered—a *victim*. The drama was between two abstractions. The event was mystified and mythologized until the actual experiences and motivations were lost.

Let us begin, therefore, by demythologizing and demystifying this all-too-typical tragedy. Let's try to unravel the experience, viewing it as a human tragedy involving real people—people who are in many ways much like us.

CHAPTER 2

The Victim

I never met this young woman. I was discouraged from doing so by the adversarial nature of the legal process, by the circumstances of my involvement in the case, and by my own uncertainty about how to proceed. In retrospect, I probably should have risked the attempt. However, let me try to project, on the basis of other victims' experiences, something of what she has gone through.[1]

The Experience

When she entered her hallway and was assaulted by a man with a knife wearing a mask, she was terrified. Her first reaction was one of shock and disbelief: "This cannot be happening to me." Some victims report that they are paralyzed initially, unable to act. She, however, screamed and struggled. She reported later that

---

1. Considerable information about the victim experience is becoming available. I have especially appreciated Morton Bard and Dawn Sangrey, *The Crime Victim's Book* (New York: Brunner-Mazel, 1986), 2d ed. See also Shelley Neiderbach, *Invisible Wounds: Crime Victims Speak* (New York: The Hayworth Press, 1986) and Doug Magee, *What Murder Leaves Behind: The Victim's Family* (New York: Dodd, Mead and Co., 1983). Charlotte Hullinger, cofounder of Parents of Murdered Children, Inc., has been an important help.

she was certain that she was going to die.

A common reaction of victims is what psychologists have called "frozen-fear compliance." Confronted by such a terrifying, overpowering situation, victims of violent crime (like victims of hijackings) frequently seem to cooperate with their oppressor. In some crimes such as rape, this natural psychological reaction may be misinterpreted by courts as willing collaboration. In actuality, however, such compliance is rooted in terror.

Once the initial attack was over, this woman did in fact react in this way. The offender's perspective was that once he realized what he had done, he tried to help her get assistance. In his view, she had cooperated. In reality, however, she was terrified of him, felt completely in his power, and therefore attempted to cooperate and pacify him in any way that she could.

During the initial "impact" phase, then, her reactions were in common with most victims: she was overwhelmed by feelings of confusion, helplessness, terror, vulnerability. Those feelings stayed with her during the coming weeks, although with less intensity. However, intense new feelings arose: anger, guilt, suspicion, depression, meaninglessness, self-doubt, regret.

During this "recoil" phase she struggled to adjust and experienced wide swings in mood. Some days she seemed to be recovering her buoyancy, her optimism, only to be followed by severe depression and/or rage. She became suspicious of other people, especially strangers, and was easily startled.

She began to have vivid and frightening dreams and fantasies uncharacteristic of her and contrary to her values. She fantasized, for instance, about taking terrible vengeance on the person who did this to her. Since this was in contrast to her values, it brought her anxiety and guilt. When awake, she often replayed what had happened and how she responded, wondering why she reacted the way she did and what she should have done differently.

Like most crime victims, she struggled with feelings of shame and of blame. She asked repeatedly why it happened, why she reacted the way she did, what she could have done differently, and was tempted to conclude that it was in some way her fault. If only she had not rebuffed him when he tried to talk with her. . . . If only she had not gone out that night. . . . Perhaps she was being punished for something she did. . . .

She will continue to grapple with feelings of fear as well as a sense of vulnerability and helplessness. Someone else took control, leaving her feeling powerless and vulnerable, and it will be difficult to recover the confidence of again being safe and in control. Accompanying this struggle will be the attempt to regain trust in others, in the world. Someone had violated her and her world, and the sense of being at home with people, with her home, with her neighborhood, with her world, will be difficult to regain.

Most victims experience intense feelings of anger: at the person who did this, at others who should have prevented it, at God who allowed or even caused it. This intense anger may contradict the values they profess, increasing their guilt. For a religious person, an experience like this often provokes a crisis of faith. Why did this happen? What did I do to deserve this? How can a loving, just God let this happen? Lack of a satisfying answer can result in a profound crisis of belief.

During the weeks following the attack this young woman struggled to adjust to her new situation. In part she was grieving: the loss of an eye, the loss of her innocence. She sought ways to deal with intense new feelings of anger, guilt, vulnerability. And she needed to readjust her vision of the world and of herself. She now sees the world as a potentially dangerous place that has betrayed her. No longer can she see it as the comfortable, predictable environment of her past. She sees herself as having been naive, needing to stop being so "nice" and trusting. Given these new feelings, she is even beginning to adjust her self-image. Although she had previously viewed herself as a caring, loving, person-oriented individual, this self-concept has now been shattered.

What about her friends in all this?

If she had been fortunate, she would have had friends, church members, co-workers, and neighbors willing to seek her out. She needed people who would accept her feelings regardless of whether they are understood, without judgment, who would listen to her story over and over. She needed friends who would help her not to blame herself for what happened or how she has responded, who would provide support and assistance without taking over for her.[2]

Unfortunately, however, her friends tend to avoid the subject. They easily tire of her story, feeling that

---

2. Charlotte Hullinger, cofounder of Parents of Murdered Children and herself a victim, has identified four ways that friends tend to respond to victims:

The Rescuer. Fear makes them want quick resolutions. Rather than listen, they make suggestions that encourge dependency. They are uncomfortable with just having victims ventilate. It is hard for them to see people in pain and to feel helpless, so they want to fix things.

The Hostile Helper. Fear makes them angry. They may want to blame the victim. They speak judgmentally and try to distance themselves from the victim. As they are afraid, they claim it would not have happened to them.

The Helpless Helper. Fear overwhelms them. They feel as bad or worse than the victim but they don't really listen. They may make the victim feel so bad that he or she becomes sorry for the helper.

The Positive Helper. This person is aware of and acknowledges fears. She or he faces vulnerability, listens without judgment, and has a sense of timing. Such helpers may say, "You must be terribly upset." "It takes time." "You handled it well." "It must be awful." In other words, they give victims permission to talk without specifying how they do so.

she needs to put this behind and move on. They admonish her not to be angry, and imply in various ways that she contributed to what happened—that she is somehow to blame. They imply that what happened was in some way God's will. Perhaps she needed to be punished. Perhaps God caused this for some good end. Perhaps God is trying to teach her a lesson. Such suggestions increase her tendency to blame herself and to question her faith.

These reactions by friends and acquaintances are examples of what psychologists have termed "secondary victimization." When we hear of a crime, when we listen to a victim relate his or her story, we too experience some of the feelings of victimization. Those are painful feelings which we like to avoid. So we avoid the subject and we tend to blame. After all, if we can locate the cause for her troubles in something she did or is, we can distance ourselves from her situation. We can believe that such a thing is not likely to happen to us. That makes us feel more secure.

She therefore had to fight for the right to grieve. Since her close friends—including perhaps a boy friend —suffered with her, additional strain was caused by the fact that they grieved differently and less apparently. Divorce rates are high among parents of murdered children, for example, in part because partners grieve differently and have different ways of adjusting. If not identified and understood, differences in ways of grieving may drive people apart.

The experience of being a crime victim can be highly intense, touching all areas of life. For this young woman, it affected her sleeping, her appetite, and her health. She turned to drugs and alcohol in order to cope. Medical costs became a significant burden. Her job performance deteriorated. Various experiences and special events continued to bring back painful memories. Had she been married, her marriage might have been strained. Her sexual interest and behavior might have been affected. For crime victims, the aftereffects often are traumatic and far-reaching.

The breadth and intensity of the crime experience is not too difficult to acknowledge in a violent crime like this one, although the full dimensions of the crisis are difficult for nonvictims to fathom. What is often overlooked is that victims of offenses which we consider less serious may experience similar reactions. In describing their experiences, victims of burglary often sound much like victims of rape. Victims of vandalism and car theft report many of the same reactions as victims of violent assault, though perhaps in less intense form.

Why So Traumatic?

Why such reactions? Why is crime so devastating, so hard to recover from? The reason is that crime is in essence a violation: a violation of the self, a desecration of who we are, of what we believe, of our private space. Crime is devastating because it upsets two fundamental assumptions on which we base our lives: our belief that the world is an orderly, meaningful place, and our belief in personal autonomy. Both assumptions are essential for wholeness.

Most of us assume that the world (or at least the part of the world in which we live) is an orderly, predictable, understandable place. Everything may not happen as we wish, but at least we can provide answers for much of what happen. Generally we know what to expect. How could we live with any sense of security otherwise?

Crime, like cancer, upsets this sense of order and meaning. Consequently, crime victims, like cancer victims, want answers. Why did this happen to me? What could I have done to prevent it? These are only a few of the questions which nag at victims. Answers to such questions are important because answers restore order and meaning. If we can provide answers to the questions of what and why, the world can make sense again. Without answers, victims tend to blame themselves, others, and God. Blame, in fact, is one important way of providing answers in order to restore meaning and some semblance of wholeness.

But to be whole we also need to have a sense of personal autonomy, of power over our own lives. To be deprived unwillingly of personal power, to be involuntarily in the control of others, is intensely degrading and dehumanizing. Crime destroys this sense of autonomy. Someone else has taken control of our lives, our property, our space. It leaves victims feeling vulnerable, defenseless, out of control, dehumanized. Here again self-blame may be a coping mechanism. If we can locate the cause of the crime in something we did, we can determine to avoid that behavior, thus regaining a sense of control.

The woman in our story was not simply the victim of a physical attack, then. She was—and is—the victim of an assault on her very sense of self, on her self-concept as an autonomous individual in a predictable world. The psychological effects may be more serious than the physical loss.

The Recovery Process

To recover, victims need to move from the "recoil" phase to a "reorganization" phase. In cases of serious crimes, they need to move from being victims to being survivors. Victims need to progress to the point where the offense and the offender no longer dominate them. However, this is difficult and time-consuming. For many people, it may never be fully attained.

What do victims need in order to recover? Any answer to this question is a bit risky. Only a victim can answer authentically, and needs vary from person to person. In general, though, the needs of crime victims include (but are not limited to) the following.

Most obviously, perhaps, victims need compensation for losses. Financial and material losses may present a real financial burden. Moreover, the symbolic value of losses may be as important or more important than the actual material losses. In either case, repayment can assist recovery. Full repayment for the material and psychological damage may well be impossible. But the sense of loss and the resulting need to have things made right in a material way can be quite acute.

No one can give back an eye to the woman in the preceding story. Restitution for expenses, however, might ease the burden. At the same time, it may provide a sense of restoration on a symbolic level.

As important as material losses are, surveys of crime victims find that they usually rate other needs more highly. One of these is the need for answers, for information. Why me? Did this person have something personal against me? Is he or she coming back? What happened to my property? What could I have done to avoid becoming a victim? Information must be provided and questions answered.

It can be suggested that to find healing, victims must find answers to six basic questions:[3]

1. What happened?
2. Why did it happen to me?

---

3. Adapted from Charles Finley, "Catastrophes: An Overview of Family Reactions," Chapter 1 of Charles Finley and Hamilton I. McCubbin, *Stress and the Family,* Vol. II: Coping with Catastrophe (New York: Brunner/Mazel, 1983).

3. Why did I act as I did at the time?
4. Why have I acted as I have since that time?
5. What if it happens again?
6. What does this mean for me and for my outlook (my faith, my vision of the world, my future)?

Some of these questions can be answered only by the victims themselves. They must, for example, find their own explanations for their behavior at the time and since that time. And they must decide how they will respond to similar situations in the future. However, the first two questions have to do with the facts of the offense. What actually happened? Why did it happen to me? Information can be very important to victims, and answers to such questions may provide an entrance on the road to recovery. Without answers to such questions, recovery may be difficult.

In addition to restitution and answers, victims need opportunities to express and validate their emotions: their anger, their fear, their pain. Even though such feelings may be hard for us to hear and may not square with what we would wish them to feel, these feelings are a natural, human response to the violation of crime. Anger, in fact, needs to be recognized as a common stage of suffering, and one that cannot simply be short-circuited. The suffering and the pain are part of the offense and need to be expressed and to be heard. Victims need opportunities and arenas to express their feelings and their suffering, but also to tell their stories. They need to have their "truth" heard and validated by others.

Victims also need to be empowered. Their sense of personal autonomy has been stolen from them by an offender, and they need to have this sense of personal power returned to them. This includes a sense of control over their environment. Thus new locks and other security devices may be important to them, or they may change their lifestyle as a means of reducing risks. Similarly, they need a sense of control or involvement in the resolution of their own cases. They need to feel that they have choices, and that these choices are real.

Victims often feel that safety is important. They want assurance that this will not happen again—to them or to others. They want to know that steps are being taken toward this end.

A common thread running throughout may be described as the need for an experience of justice. For some victims, this may take the form of a demand for vengeance. However, a demand for retribution may itself grow out of a victim's failure to have a more positive experience of justice. Indeed, an experience of justice is so basic that without it, healing may be well impossible.

An experience of justice for victims has many dimensions, some of which have already been suggested. Victims need assurance that what happened to them was wrong, unfair, undeserved. They need opportunities to speak the truth of what happened to them, including their suffering. They need to be heard and affirmed. People working with women who are victims of domestic violence have summarized these needs in terms such as "truth-telling," "breaking the silence," "deprivatization," and "deminimization."

As part of this experience of justice, victims need to know that steps are being taken to rectify the wrong and to reduce the opportunities for it to recur. As noted earlier, they may want restitution, not just for the material recovery involved but for the moral statement implied in the recognition that the act was wrongful and in the attempt to make things right.

Justice may be a state of affairs, but it is also an experience. Justice must be experienced as real. Victims are not usually content to be assured that things are being taken care of. They want to be informed and, at least at certain points, to be consulted and involved.

Crime may upset our sense of meaning, which is a basic human need. Consequently the path to recovery involves a search for meaning. Indeed, the six questions that victims must answer in order to recover involve a search for meaning. For crime victims, the need for justice is most basic because, as philosopher and historian Michael Ignatieff has observed, justice provides a framework of meanings that makes sense of experience.[4] All of this leads me to several observations.

First, victimization can be a highly traumatic experience. It is so because it is a violation of something very basic: our vision of ourselves as autonomous individuals in a meaningful world. It is also a violation of trust in our relationships with others.

Second, this is often true not only for violent crimes such as murder and rape which most of us view as serious, but also for crimes such as spouse abuse, burglary, vandalism, or car theft—offenses which society often treats as minor.

Third, common patterns of victim response emerge, taking into account variations in personality, situation, and offense. Certain feelings such as fear and anger are nearly universal, for example, and many victims appear to move through identifiable stages of adjustment.

Finally, being victimized by another person generates a series of needs which, if met, can assist in the recovery process. For the unattended victim, however, healing may be very difficult and incomplete.

---

4. Michael Ignatieff, "Imprisonment and the Need for Justice," an address to the 1987 Canadian Criminal Justice Congress in Toronto. An edited version is printed in *Liaison*, January 1988.

Our Response

It would seem logical, given all this, that victims would be at the center of the justice process with their needs as a major focus. One might suppose that victims would have some say in what charges are brought and that they and their needs might be taken into account in the final disposition of the case. One could at least expect that they would be told when an offender has been identified and would be kept informed as the case moves through the court. In many cases, however, little or none of this happens. Victims have little say as to whether or how the case is prosecuted. Often they are taken into account only if they are needed as witnesses. Rarely are they notified when an offender is apprehended. Only where it is required by law do courts make any regular effort to notify victims of the process of the case through the court or to solicit their input into the final disposition.

This was illustrated graphically by a woman at a seminar which I once helped lead. I had spent some time describing the situation of crime victims—their suffering, their needs, their omission from the "justice" process—when a woman near the back stood up and said, "You are right. On one occasion my house was burglarized. On another I was assaulted in a dark street. In neither case was I informed or consulted until the case was through or nearly through the courts. And do you know what? I am the prosecutor! My own staff did not keep me informed." You can imagine, then, what the rest of us can expect.

This realization often comes to victims soon after they report an offense. They are frequently astonished to find that charges can be either pursued or dropped without regard to victims' wishes and that they are provided little information about the case.

Such neglect of victims not only fails to meet their

needs: it compounds the injury. Many speak of a "second victimization" by criminal justice personnel and processes. The question of personal power is central here. Part of the dehumanizing nature of victimization by crime is the way it robs victims of power. Instead of returning power to them by allowing them to participate in the justice process, the legal system compounds the injury by again denying power. Instead of helping, the process hurts.

In the U.S., federal legislation has been passed to help support victim assistance and compensation programs which have begun in many states. Compensation programs allow victims of serious personal crimes who meet a variety of fairly stiff criteria to apply for reimbursement for expenses. Victim assistance programs, in communities where they exist, provide counseling and other resources for victims. England has led in the development of local victim support programs which use volunteers to provide support and assistance to victims as they proceed through the justice process and seek recovery.[5]

All of this helps, indicating a new and important concern for victims. Unfortunately, though, these efforts remain mere beginnings, veritable drops in the bucket, when compared to the needs. Victims still remain peripheral to the justice process. In the legal process, victims represent footnotes to the crime.

Our failure to take victims seriously leaves a terrible legacy of fear, suspicion, anger, and guilt. It leads to persistent and perhaps growing demands for vengeance. It encourages the building of stereotypes. (How

---

5. National Association of Victim Support Schemes, 39 Brixton Rd., London SW9 6DZ, England. In the U.S., the National Organization for Victim Assistance (NOVA, 1757 Park Rd. N.W., Washington, DC 20010) serves as a national clearinghouse.

else, after all, is one to make sense of an offender one has not met?) And these stereotypes lead to further distrust, encouraging racism and classism.

Perhaps worst of all, from the point of view of the victim, is the lack of closure. When victims are unattended and their needs unmet, they often find it difficult to put the experience behind them. Victims often relate their experiences vividly, as if they happened yesterday, when in fact they may have happened years ago. Nothing in their experience has let them really overcome. Instead, the experience and the offender still dominate their lives. The victim is still denied power. And the damage is not limited to individual victims; it is shared by friends and by others who hear about the tragedy. The open wounds result in increased suspicion, fear, anger, and feelings of vulnerability throughout the community. Indeed, they work to undermine a sense of community.

This failure to attend to victims' needs does not mean that we will never mention victims in the legal process or in the news, however. On the contrary, we may invoke their names to do all sorts of things to the offender, regardless of what victims actually want. The reality is that we do almost nothing directly for the victim, in spite of the rhetoric. We do not listen to what they have suffered and what they need. We do not seek to give them back some of what they have lost. We do not let them help to decide how the situation should be resolved. We do not help them to recover. We may not even let them know what has transpired since the offense!

This, then, is the ultimate irony, the ultimate tragedy. Those who have most directly suffered are not to be part of the resolution of the offense. In fact, as we shall see, victims are not even part of our understanding of the problem.

CHAPTER 3

The Offender

I have suggested that the wounded victim in our opening story probably has not experienced justice. But what has been happening to the young offender who attacked her?

He has been through an elaborate and lengthy process in which one professional—a lawyer—who is expected to represent his interests has been pitted against another professional—the prosecutor—who represents the state and its interests. This process is guided by an elaborate labyrinth of rules called "due process." These are designed to protect both his and society's (but not necessarily the victim's) rights. Through this process, a series of professionals (prosecutor, judge, probation officers, psychiatrists) have helped to decide that he is in fact guilty of the offense as defined by law. This has included a determination not only that he committed a legally defined offense, but that he intended to do so. The judge has also determined what should be done with him.

Throughout this process, the offender has been almost a bystander. His primary focus has been on his own situation and future. Almost inevitably he has become preoccupied by the various obstacles, decisions, and stages that need to be faced. Nevertheless, most of the decisions have been made for him by others.

The Prison Experience

Now he is in prison. While the length of the term commonly assessed in the U.S. may seem unusual in a Canadian or Western European setting, the decision to imprison is not. In fact, prison is the normal response to crime in contemporary Western society. We operate under a presumption of prison. Prison is not a sentence of last resort which must be justified and rationalized by the judge which imposes it. On the contrary, prison is normative, and judges find it necessary to explain and rationalize a sentence other than prison.

This presumption of prison explains why our incarceration rates are so high. Americans often believe that we are "soft on crime." While it is true that there are individual cases and jurisdictions where offenders may seem to "get off easy," as a nation the reality is quite different. By international standards, we are very harsh. American incarceration rates are much higher per capita than those of any other industrialized nation, with the exception of Russia and South Africa. Some observers have suggested that if political prisoners were excluded from the statistics of the latter countries, the U.S. would stand alone.

Prison is the sentence of first, not last, resort, and this is true not only for violent crimes. Many international observers are surprised to learn that many if not most of the prisoners being held in American prisons are serving sentences for property crimes. American imprisonment rates are high because we consider prison sentences as our norm.

When sentencing the offender, the judge in our case expressed the hope that this young offender would learn nonviolent patterns of behavior while in prison. What, in fact, is he likely to learn?

By now, this young man may well have become the victim of violence himself. What lesson is he learning? He will learn that conflict is normal, that violence is the great problem solver, that one must be violent in order to survive, that one responds to frustration with violence. That is, after all, normal in the distorted world of prison.

This young man's age and small physical stature make it likely that he will become the victim of not just violence, but sexual violence. Homosexual rape of young men is frequent in prison, where older, patterned offenders are often mixed in with younger, less experienced, men. Such rape may reflect the prolonged sexual deprivation and frustration characteristic of prison life. More often, though, rape becomes a distorted means of asserting power over others by persons denied legitimate forms of power and meaning. Homosexual rape in prison is also a vehicle for expressing contempt, for degrading others. This in turn reflects disturbing—but all-too-common—understandings of masculinity and femininity. Given this young man's apparent insecurity, it is likely that his sense of self-worth and manhood will be severely damaged and distorted by this experience.

So much, then, for the judge's hope that patterns of violence will be forgotten. On the contrary, the judge has ordered this offender to live for at least twenty years in an atmosphere which nourishes and teaches violence. Violence may become for him a way of coping, a way of solving problems, a way of communicating.

This offender got in trouble in part because of a poor sense of self-worth and of personal autonomy, personal power. Yet the prison experience will further strip away his sense of worth and of autonomy, leaving him with even fewer resources for obtaining a sense of worth and autonomy in legitimate ways.

I am convinced that much crime and violence is a way of asserting personal identity and power. This was expressed well by a friend who spent 17 years in prison for a series of armed robberies. Finally, through the help of patient church people, he made the transition to society. Bobby had grown up black and poor. His father, a janitor and an alcoholic, felt locked into a world that became a prison with little hope for escape. Crime was, for Bobby, an escape from the prison of personal nothingness. "At least when I had a shotgun in my hand I was somebody!" Bobby told me. How could he respect others when his respect for himself was so poor?

Psychologist Robert Johnson, writing about murderers on death row, has captured well the meaning and roots of violence.

> Their violence is not a specter or disease that afflicts them without rhyme or reason, nor is it merely a convenient vehicle for ugly passions. Rather, their violence is an adaptation to bleak and often brutal lives. . . . [The violence] of most violent men is ultimately spawned by the hostility and abuse of others, and it feeds on low self-confidence and fractured self-esteem. Paradoxically, their violence is a twisted form of self-defense that serves only to confirm the feelings of weakness and vulnerability that provoke it in the first place. When their violence claims innocent victims, it signals not a triumph of nerve but a loss of control.[1]

---

1. Robert Johnson, "A Life for a Life?" *Justice Quarterly*, 1, No. 4 (December 1984), 571.

Given the poor sense of self-worth and of personal autonomy characteristic of so many offenders, petty arguments and conflicts in prison often lead quickly to major violence. An argument over a dollar can easily lead to death.

Our offender may have gotten in trouble because of a poor sense of self-worth and of personal power. His offense may have been a distorted attempt to say he was someone and to assert some control over his life and perhaps others. Yet the prison setting will further strip away his sense of power and worth.

The entire prison setting is structured to dehumanize. Prisoners are given numbers, standardized clothing, and little or no personal space. They are denied almost all possibilities for personal decision and power. Indeed, the focus of the entire setting is on obedience, on learning to take orders. In that situation, a person has few choices. He or she can learn to obey, to be submissive. This is the response the prison system encourages, yet it is the response least likely to encourage a successful transition to free society. Our offender got into trouble because of his inability to be self-governing, to take charge of his own life in a legitimate way. Prison will further deprive him of that ability. Thus it should not be surprising that those who conform to prison rules best are *not* those who make the most successful transition into the community after prison.

A second response when confronted by pressure to conform is to rebel. Many do. In part, such rebellion is an attempt to retain a sense of individuality. As a category, those who rebel seem to make the transition to free society better than those who conform (although rebellion may make release on parole more unlikely). There are exceptions: if the rebellion is too violent or too prolonged, a pattern of rebellion and violence may begin to dominate.

Jack Abbott is a prisoner who has spent most of his life fighting conformity in prison. His book, *In the Belly of the Beast*, is an articulate, insightful look at the world of prison.[2] After years in prison he was released, only to kill again when he perceived that he had been insulted.

A third option is to become devious, to appear to conform while finding ways to retain areas of personal freedom. This leads to another lesson learned in prison: the lesson that manipulation is normal. That is, after all, how one copes in prison. And it is how prison authorities manage prisoners. How else, after all, can such few authorities manage so many prisoners, given such limited resources? In short, the convict learns to con.

Our offender got into trouble because of his inability to make good choices. The ability to make his own good choices will be further eroded by the prison experience. During his twenty or more years he will have little encouragement or even opportunity to make choices and take responsibility. In fact, what he will learn is dependence. During those years he will not pay rent, will not have to manage money, will not be primarily responsible for a family. He will be dependent upon the state to take care of him. And when he emerges, he will have few coping skills. How will he learn to keep a job, to save, to budget, to pay bills?

In prison our offender will absorb a warped ideal of interpersonal relationships. Domination over others will be the goal, whether over a marriage partner, a friend, or a business acquaintance. Caring will be seen

---

2. Jack Henry Abbott, *In the Belly of the Beast: Letters from Prison* (New York: Random House, 1981).

as a weakness. And the weak are meant to be preyed upon.

This offender needs to learn that he is someone of worth, that he has the power and responsibility to make good choices. He needs to learn respect for others and their property. He needs to learn to cope peacefully with frustration and conflict. He needs coping skills. Instead, he will be encouraged to turn to violence for personal validation, as a means to cope, as a way to solve problems. His sense of worth and autonomy will either be weakened or become based on dangerous foundations.

When examined in this context, then, the judge's hope becomes incredibly naive and wrongheaded.

Will prison teach him nonviolent patterns of behavior? Hardly. It is more likely to make him even more violent. Will it protect society from him? For a while, perhaps, but eventually he will come out, and he may be worse for the wear. And while there, he may become a danger to fellow inmates.

Will it deter? Whether his imprisonment will discourage others from committing similar crimes is debatable, but it is unlikely to deter him. Indeed, as I have already suggested, he may be more, not less, likely to commit crimes because of the lack of coping skills and the patterns of behavior he will learn in prison. Moreover, the threat of prison will no longer hold such terror for him since he will know he can survive there. Indeed, after twenty years it will be home and he will feel insecure outside.

Some prisoners who have spent that long inside commit crimes upon release precisely so they can go back to a place that is familiar. They would rather be where they have the skills to cope than face the uncertainties and dangers of life on the outside. Recently I was a guest at a group meeting in a British day center for ex-offenders. One of the young men participating had been in prison a number of times. "I like being out," he said, "but I'm just as happy inside." The threat of prison can hardly deter such an individual.

Nor is the threat of prison likely to deter people who are poor and marginal, who believe life on the outside to be a kind of prison. To a person in such a situation, to be sentenced to prison is simply to exchange one kind of confinement for another. Yet we reserve prison sentences primarily for the poor and the powerless.

What Needs to Happen?

When sentencing this young man, the judge spoke of the need to hold offenders accountable. Most of us would agree. Offenders do indeed need to be held accountable for their behavior. But what does accountability mean? For this judge, and for most people today, accountability for offenders means that the offender must experience punitive consequences—often prison —whether for deterrence or for punishment. "Making people accountable" means forcing people to "take their medicine"—an odd metaphor for anything as damaging as prison.

This is an extremely limited and abstract understanding of accountability. Without an intrinsic link between the act and the consequences, true accountability is hardly possible. And as long as consequences are decided *for* offenders, accountability will not involve responsibility.

In order to commit offenses and live with their behavior, offenders often construct elaborate rationalizations for their actions, and prison gives them much time and encouragement to do so. They come to believe that what they did was not too serious, that the victim "deserved" it, that everyone is doing it, that insurance will take care of any losses. They find ways to divert blame from themselves to other people and situations. They also employ stereotypes about victims and potential victims. Unconsciously or even consciously they work to insulate themselves from the victim. Some burglars even report that they turn photographs toward the wall in homes they burglarize so that they will not have to think of the victims.

Nothing in our criminal justice process ever challenges these "misattributions." On the contrary, the process often encourages rationalizations and strengthens stereotypes. The adversarial nature of the process tends to harden stereotypes about victims and about society. The intricate, painful, nonparticipatory nature of the process encourages a tendency to focus on the wrongs experienced by the offender, diverting attention from the harm done to the victim. Many, if not most, offenders end up feeling that they have been treated badly (and they may well have!). This in turn helps them focus on their own plight rather than that of the victim. At minimum, because the criminal process is so complex and so offender-oriented, they are caught up entirely in their own legal situations.

Consequently, offenders rarely are encouraged or allowed to see the real human costs of what they have done. What is it really like to have one's home burglarized or car stolen, to experience the fear and questions about who did this and why? What is it like to believe you are going to die and then to lose an eye? What kind of person is the victim? Nothing in an offender's experience with justice addresses those issues. Nothing forces him or her to face up to their rationalizations and stereotypes. In the case above, the offender made some attempt to understand what he did, but his understanding is incomplete and will soon be blotted out by his experience of justice and punishment.

Genuine accountability, then, includes an opportunity to understand the human consequences of one's acts, to face up to what one has done and to whom one has done it. But real accountability involves more. Accountability also involves taking responsibility for the results of one's behavior. Offenders must be allowed and encouraged to help decide what will happen to make things right, then to take steps to repair the damage.

Judge Dennis Challeen points out that the problem with most sentences is that although they make offenders accountable (in the sense of taking their punishment) they do not make offenders responsible. Yet a lack of responsibility is what got them into trouble in the first place. When punishment is handed down to responsible people, Challeen argues, they often respond responsibly. When we hand down sanctions to those who are irresponsible, however, it tends to make them more irresponsible.[3]

Some courts have begun to introduce restitution to victims into sentences. This is a step in the right direction. However, the rationale for restitution has often been fuzzy and misplaced. Often it is viewed as a way of punishing the offender rather than a way of making things right to the victim. Also, it is usually an imposed sanction and thus does not encourage offenders' ownership in the outcome. Usually the offender does not participate in the restitution decision and has little or no understanding of the victim's losses. He or she thus is likely to view restitution as one more punitive sanction rather than as a logical attempt to right a

3. Dennis A. Challeen, *Making It Right: A Common Sense Approach to Criminal Justice* (Aberdeen, South Dakota: Melius and Peterson Publishing, 1986).

wrong and fulfill an obligation to another person. Restitution sentences which are imposed on offenders as punishment are unlikely to help them be responsible. This is a major reason for poor repayment rates in some restitution programs.

Our offender needs to be held accountable for his behavior in whatever ways he can. This means that he must be encouraged to develop as complete an understanding as possible of what he has done (i.e., what his actions have meant to the other person involved, and to acknowledge his role in it). He must also be allowed and encouraged to make things right to the extent that it is possible to do so. And he should participate in finding ways that this can be done. That is real accountability.

Such accountability may help bring resolution to the victim by meeting some of her needs. It can also help to bring resolution to the offender. An understanding of what hurt he has caused may help discourage him from causing such harm in the future. An opportunity to make things right, to become a productive citizen, can boost his self-esteem and thus encourage lawful behavior.

What Will Happen?

None of this is likely to happen to our offender during the next twenty years. The result?

He will have no opportunity to confront the stereotypes and rationalizations that have led up to his offense. Indeed, they will be amplified and elaborated upon during his years in prison. He will have no opportunity to build the interpersonal skills, the coping skills, that he will need to live successfully on the outside. In fact, he will learn the wrong interpersonal skills and will lose what coping skills he has. He will

have no way to face up to what he has done or to
make things right.

He will have no way to deal with the guilt that such
an offense causes. There is no place in the process
where he can be forgiven, where he can feel he has
made things right. Imagine the effect on his self-image.
His alternatives are few. He can avoid the issue, ration-
alizing his behavior. He can turn his anger on himself
and contemplate suicide. He can turn his anger on
others. In any case, he will continue to be defined as
an offender, long after he has "paid his debt" by taking
his punishment. The hatred and violence bred in him
in prison may come to replace any sorrow and grief he
may have had.

Like the victim, he will have no opportunity for closure, for putting this behind. The wound will continue
to be rubbed raw.

By his actions, our offender has violated another
person. He has also violated relationships of trust within a community. Nothing in the process of justice will
help him comprehend these dimensions of what he has
done, however.

The offense was committed by a person who himself
had been violated. While not excusable on these
grounds, his actions grew out of a history of abuse. As
a child, he was physically abused. As an adult, he was
psychologically and spiritually abused, which wounded
his sense of himself and his relationship to the world.
Nothing in the process will take that into account.
Nothing is likely to start him on the road to wholeness.

CHAPTER 4

Some Common Themes

Although I have looked at victim and offender separately, some common themes emerge.

Repentance and Forgiveness

So far I have analyzed their experiences and their needs primarily in experiential and psychological terms. Let us look briefly at their dilemma in Christian terms.

Both of the young people in the case I have described need to be healed. For genuine healing to take place, at least two preconditions need to be met: repentance and forgiveness.

If healing is to occur, it is helpful for victims to be able to forgive.

From a theological perspective, that seems rather straightforward: we are called to forgive our enemies, those who harm us, because God has forgiven us. We cannot be free as long as we are dominated by enmity. We must follow God's example.

From a practical, experiential point of view, that seems very difficult, perhaps impossible. How can a mother or father forgive a person who has killed their child? How is it possible to move beyond feelings of anger and revenge? How dare someone who has not experienced it even suggest such a thing? Can forgiveness be considered until safety is assured? Is such reassurance possible?

To forgive and be forgiven is not easy, and cannot be suggested glibly. Nor should those who cannot find it in themselves to forgive be encouraged to feel an extra burden of guilt. Real forgiveness cannot simply be willed or forced, but must come in its own time, with God's help.[1] Forgiveness is a gift. It should not be made into a burden.[2]

It is important to clarify our understanding of forgiveness. Often we think forgiveness means forgetting what happened, writing it off, perhaps letting the victimizer off the hook easily. But forgiveness does not mean forgetting what happened. This young woman will never—and should never—completely forget her trauma and her loss. She should not be expected to. Nor does forgiveness mean redefining the offense as a nonoffense. It does not mean saying, "It wasn't so bad, it doesn't matter." It was bad, it does matter, and to deny that is to devalue both the experience of suffering

---

1. I have found Marie Marshall Fortune's work helpful on forgiveness. See, for example, *Sexual Violence: The Unmentionable Sin* (New York: Pilgrim Press, 1983), and "Justice-Making in the Aftermath of Woman-Battering," in *Domestic Violence on Trial*, ed. Daniel Sonkin (New York: Springer Publishers, 1987), pp. 237-248. Cf. Jeffrie G. Murphy and Jean Hampton, *Forgiveness and Mercy* (Cambridge, England: Cambridge University Press, 1988) and Thomas R. Yoder Neufeld, "Forgiveness and the Dangerous Few: The Biblical Basis," address to the Christian Council for Reconciliation, Montreal, Quebec, November 18, 1983.

Morton MacCullum-Paterson has suggested that forgiveness may involve a willingness to give up the intention to inflict vengeance. It may involve a willingness to turn the issue over to God for forgiveness. The root meaning of the word *forgive* in the New Testament, he points out, is to hand over or set aside. See *Toward a Justice That Heals* (Toronto: The United Church Publishing House, 1988), p. 56.

2. Thanks to Dave Worth for this helpful distinction.

and the very humanity of the person responsible.

Forgiveness is letting go of the power the offense and the offender have over a person. It means no longer letting that offense and offender dominate. Without this experience of forgiveness, without this closure, the wound festers, the violation takes over our consciousness, our lives. It, and the offender, are in control. Real forgiveness, then, is an act of empowerment and healing. It allows one to move from victim to survivor.

It is possible to move from victim to survivor in other ways. Some victims attempt to do this by "living well," feeling that to live successfully after a tragedy is the best revenge. "I'll show them" is the approach, and it is not without psychological value. But this method of coping still puts the offense and the offender at the center. Forgiveness, on the other hand, allows the experience to become part of one's life story, part of one's biography in an important way, but without letting it continue to control.

Certain conditions help forgiveness to happen. An expression of responsibility, regret, and repentance on the part of an offender can be a powerful help. An essential condition for most people, however, is support from others and an experience of justice. Prayer is an important part of this "healing of memories." A person or group in a pastoring role can hear confession and offer absolution. All of us, and especially our congregations, have a responsibility to encourage an environment where this can happen.

As I suggested earlier, an experience of justice has many dimensions. One of these dimensions is captured in the biblical concept of lament, expressed in some of the psalms. Speaking to the church, theologian Walter Brueggemann has described it well.

The way we move to maturity is to bring all the nega-
tivities to full speech. I can see the priest standing by and
saying: have you got it all out yet, is there anymore? And
I discover that if I get [it] out in structured ways wherein
it can be received, I really do walk away new and free.
But if we do not practice lament, if we do not practice
speech that brings it to the throne of God, I have to sit on
it and carry it around with me for the rest of my life. We
live in a world of people who are waiting for a chance to
speak it into God's Holy Ear. The mystery is that if you
say it honestly to God, God is not frightened off, offended, or alienated, but rather God draws nearer. . . . *Very
many people in our repressed culture need constant permission
to speak their rage, hatreds, hurts, fears.* People are not likely
to sing hymns of praise with the same freedom, power,
and energy if they have not been through the full statement of their loss and hurt and grief before they get
there. The pastoral task is to authorize people to do the
kinds of speech that will make the job possible. . . .

*The church's business is not to say something good but to say
the truth. Sometimes the only truth is that it hurts.* Psalm 88
is a psalm for those times. The only truth that this psalm
can muster tonight is that it hurts and you better give the
wound air. The next day it may be time for some oint-
ment but not until you've given the wound some air.
Psalm 88 does not flinch before the painful truth that
there are pieces of life that are unutterable.[3]

The church has a critical responsibility in this process. Unfortunately, too often it has wanted to avoid
the pain, to dispense with the lament. But at the same

---

3. From a 1980 workshop on the Psalms presented in Toronto, Ontario.
Quoted in "A Reflective Analysis on Reconciliaton as It Relates to Criminal
Justice," an unpublished discussion paper prepared by a working group of
the National Associations Active in Criminal Justice for a May 1987 workshop in Ottawa, Canada.

time it has pressured victims to forgive. It has been reluctant to forgive victims for their natural feelings of anger and hostility toward the offender, toward society, and toward God.

If the victim needs an experience of forgiveness, so also does the offender. How else will he be able to find resolution to his guilt? How else will it be possible for him to move on to new life? How else can he develop a healthy sense of identity and self-worth? How else can he be saved?

Contrary to popular belief, offenders often do feel guilt for what they have done. Yet a sense of guilt can be terribly threatening to one's sense of self-worth and self-identity. One study has concluded that offenders are characterized by tremendous fears and that their greatest fear is of the "zero-state," that is of personal worthlessness.[4] Consequently, offenders utilize a variety of defensive techniques to avoid guilt and maintain their sense of self-worth.

One method is to develop what Michael Ignatieff has termed "exculpatory strategies" to deflect or deny their guilt.[5] They may argue, for example, that "everyone does it," that the victim "deserved" or could afford the losses, that they were provoked beyond reason. They may adopt the language of the social and psychological determinism arguing that "I'm depraved because I'm deprived." Similarly, the tendency of offenders to be obsessed with the injustices which they feel themselves to experience may be a way of insulating themselves from the burdens of guilt.

In order to live with themselves, some offenders

---

4. See David Kelley, "Stalking the Criminal Mind: Psychopaths, 'Moral Imbeciles,' and Free Will," *Harper's*, August 1985.

5. Ignatieff, "Imprisonment and the Need for Justice."

even develop elaborate fantasies about who they are and what they did. Some almost become two personalities by drawing a strict line between the guilty person and the other part of themselves.

I'm convinced that guilt is behind much of the anger which offenders express. Guilt which is accepted becomes anger at oneself. Guilt which is denied can become anger at others. Either way, such anger can be very destructive.

Some argue that guilt must be relieved through punishment. By accepting one's punishment, the debt is paid and the guilt ended. Whether or not that is true in theory, however, things do not usually work out that way in reality. If punishment is to relieve guilt, it must be felt to be legitimate and deserved. Such is rarely the case in real life. Furthermore, the idea that the offense is against society and that a debt is owed to society rarely makes sense to offenders. It is too abstract and their own identification with society is too limited.

We lack the rituals which acknowledge that the debt is paid and that the guilt has been ended. As Ignatieff points out, forgiveness would exonerate the debt as well as or better than punishment. However, we assume that we must punish before forgiveness is possible. In practice we administer punishment in such a way that it damages and feels undeserved, then deny opportunities for forgiveness.

New life requires both forgiveness and confession. For offenders to be truly whole, they must confess wrongdoing, admitting their responsibility and acknowledging the harm done. Only then is it possible to repent, to turn one's life around and begin in a new direction. Confession followed by repentance is a key to healing for offenders, but they can also bring healing for victims.

None of this—repentance, confession, and forgive-

ness by God or by the victim—eliminates the consequences of the offender's actions. Grace is not cheap.
Responsibilities to the victim remain. Nevertheless, salvation and freedom are indeed possible.

The road to such salvation, according to many chap-
lains and prison visitors, lies in the recognition of
one's utter sinfulness and worthlessness because sin is
seen as rooted in self-love.[6]

Offenders do often lack a certain moral sense, defined as a preoccupation with their own needs and an
ability to empathize with others. However, I have suggested that this preoccupation with self actually is
based in a weak self-image, perhaps in self-hate. If that
is the case, a precondition for healing may be an
awareness that they are loved and of value rather than
further confirmation of their worthlessness.

Both victim and offender need to be healed, in short,
and this healing requires opportunities for forgiveness,
confession, repentance, and reconciliation. Some of this
must take place between individuals and their God,
their church, and their community. But involved also is
the relationship between victim and offender, a relationship which if it did not exist before the offense,
does exist now.

Unfortunately, however, our present system of criminal law encourages none of this. In fact, the system discourages the processes of reconciliation. The legal process itself has no real place for repentance and certainly not for forgiveness. Moreover, by its nature it encourages offenders to deny their guilt and to focus on
their own situations. It actively seeks to keep victim
and offender apart, encouraging them to be adversaries

---

6. See Gerald Austin McHugh, *Christian Faith and Criminal Justice: Toward a Christian Response to Crime and Punishment* (New York: Paulist Press, 1978), pp. 172ff.

and discouraging them from finding a common understanding of the offense and its resolution.

The latter point was illustrated by a young ex-offender I met years ago. While serving time in prison, he had become a Christian. When he was released by the parole board, he reports that they warned him, "We understand that you have become a Christian. That may mean that you want to go back and try to make things right to the victim. If you so much as go near the victim, you will be back here immediately!" An understandable reaction, perhaps, but also a tragedy.

The Issue of Power

The issue of personal power and autonomy is central to the phenomena of crime and of justice as they are experienced by both victim and offender.

Denial of victims' autonomy by offenders is in large part what makes being a victim so traumatic. To be whole, we need some sense of being in control of our own lives and destinies. To have that taken away suddenly, arbitrarily, frighteningly, is intensely dehumanizing. Offenders turn victims into objects, into "things," robbing them of power over their own lives. This is deeply degrading.

When people are deprived of something as basic as the sense of autonomy, they seek ways to reassert it. Victims need to regain this sense, and they do so in a variety of ways. For some, it is regained simply by overcoming, by living successfully, by becoming a survivor. For some, it is done by taking safeguards or otherwise finding ways to make their life their own again. Some attempt to meet it by demands for revenge and punishment. Some are able to find empowerment through an act of Christian forgiveness. At any rate, the issue of personal power—its deprivation and its reassertion—is fundamental to the victim experience.

This issue is at the heart of the offender experience as well. Many people feel powerless and worthless. In our society, this deprivation of a sense of personal power is experienced by young men as an assault on their masculinity, since masculinity and power are often equated. One way to satisfy this thirst for autonomy and to respond to a sense of being "victimized" by a society is to find another victim to dominate. Homosexual rape in prison is just such a phenomenon. But much crime is a distorted way of asserting one's power and worth, a clumsy way of trying to assert and express oneself.

Do people in our society really have as little power as I have suggested? Certainly that assertion runs contrary to the American myth of rewards for individual ability. All those with ability who are willing to work hard can make something of themselves. If they do not, the fault is theirs. Moreover, their success is measured in material terms. Power and wealth are the basic measures of success and thus of worth. But regardless of whether this myth of individual choice and reward is true—and it is doubtful that this is the case for many—few poor people *believe* it is, at least for them.

I have often thought that the real dividing line between lower and middle-upper classes in our society has less to do with education and wealth per se than it does with the sense of choice, of power. Most of us who grow up among middle and upper class families grow up believing that we are basically masters of our own fate. While there may be obstacles, and while luck or providence plays its role, we believe that we do in fact have real choices, some real power to determine our destinies.

Many poor people do not believe this. In their view, what happens to them is due more to chance than to anything they did. If success comes, it is associated more with luck than hard work. If they are arrested for an offense, it has more to do with luck than something they did. Whether or not they do have the power to make real choices, many do not *believe* that they do, and that is what is significant. For some people, then, crime can be a way of asserting a sense of control they feel to be lacking otherwise.

Many people believe that things happen to them rather than that they control their future. This belief has important implications for the idea of deterrence. For deterrence to work, people have to believe that their actions are based on choices which in turn affect what happens to them. But Parker Rossman's interviews with young people in conflict with the law in New York provide a different picture.[7]

Every day these young people saw innocent people being arrested. Every day they saw people who were guilty going free. In their mind, there was little relationship between offense and punishment. Rather, they saw punishment like rain. Some days it rains, some days it doesn't. The rain falls on the just and unjust alike. Most of them expected to experience arrest and punishment during their lives. Like the rest of their future, it was something that just happened under the control of largely irresistible forces.

Many people in our society lack a sense of personal power, and crime can be a way of asserting such power. In that context, our prescription for those who take away another's power in order to assert their own is bizarre: we further rob them of a sense of autonomy. The entire judicial system is designed to do just that

---

7. Parker Rossman, *After Punishment What?* (Cleveland, Ohio: Collins, 1980).

by impressing offenders with the power of the state and their own lack of power. They are treated as pawns in the process. Then they are sent to prison where they are further deprived of a sense of power and worth unless they can derive some from the warped subculture of prison. So they resist "correction" for the same reason victims resist victimization: because they are being denied a sense of autonomy. How can we expect, then, that prisoners will emerge with a sense of worth that does not depend upon dominating others?[8]

Victims, too, are denied power through the criminal justice process. Their needs are ignored and they are left out of the process, thus deepening their sense of victimization.

Both victim and offender are denied power in the criminal justice process, with harmful consequences to both. But the one-sidedness of power in the process has other implications as well. A concentration of power can intoxicate individuals, making them act as if they are above the law. This concentration of power, combined with differences in education and social status, often discourages people in key roles from identifying with the powerless, whether victim or offender. They are often unwilling to listen to perspectives other than their own. The centralization of power in prosecutor and judge can intensify the problem.

In short, crime may be a way for offenders to assert power, thus to gain a sense of personal worth. In their crime, however, they rob victims of their sense of personal power. For victims to regain wholeness, this sense of autonomy must be returned. For offenders to be whole, they must develop a sense of autonomy that

8. Especially helpful on the question of power is Richard Korn, "Crime, Criminal Justice, and Corrections," *University of San Francisco Law Review*, October 1971.

is not based on overpowering others. Yet the criminal justice process compounds the problem, robbing both victim and offender of a legitimate sense of power, while concentrating power dangerously in the hands of a few.

Now let's explore the parallels between victim and offender experiences in somewhat different terms.

Judge Challeen has noted that one characteristic of many of the offenders who appear before him is that, by society's standards, they are losers.[9] People who see themselves as losers are more likely than others to assert their identities through crime. They are also less likely to be deterred by the fear of consequences. Deterrence, Challeen concludes, works least for those who need it the most: those who are losing, who have the least to lose, who are least likely to be concerned about the effects of apprehension and punishment.

Turning to victims, Norwegian criminologist Nils Christie has pointed out that victimization in itself is not "a thing."[10] Rather, it has to do with participants' interpretations of situations. Given the same experience, some people might define themselves as victims. Others might define themselves as losers. Still others might interpret themselves as victors. Just how a "victim" interprets the situation depends upon a number of factors. If such people can identify that they have been wronged and can identify how they were wronged and by whom, they may be likely to identify themselves as victims. On the other hand, some are used to losing, to being victims. If they cannot clearly

9. Dennis A. Challeen, *Making It Right* (Aberdeen, South Dakota: Milieus and Peterson Publishing, 1986), pp. 21ff. and 43ff.

10. Nils Christie, "The Ideal Victim." Unpublished lecture given at the 33d International Course in Criminology, Vancouver, British Columbia.

identify how they have been wronged and by whom, they may interpret the same experience as another loss, more evidence that they are losers.

Both Christie and sociologists Richard Sennett and Jonathan Cobb have suggested that our society tends to encourage people at the bottom to see themselves as losers rather than as victims.[11] Working class children tend to see their defeats not as evidence of the social constraints upon them but as personal failures. Poor people especially, therefore, often develop self-definitions of themselves as losers.

People who identify themselves as losers may commit crimes as a way of asserting and empowering themselves. However, because they are used to believing that they do not have the power to determine their futures and that what happens to them "just happens," they are unlikely to be deterred by the threat of punishment. The result? The creation of another class of victims: crime victims.

Some of these victims will identify themselves as crime victims, but some will not. Persons who are used to misfortune and who experience crime daily are likely to see themselves as losers, to view life as being beyond their control, to see crime as one more misfortune. The victimization simply confirms their plight. From this group may come more offenders. The cycle is repeated.

The Mystification of Crime

The case of the young man who robbed and wounded a young woman received considerable attention in its community. Like most such cases, however, the

---

11. Jonathan Cobb and Richard Sennett, *Hidden Injury of Class* (New York: Cambridge University Press, 1977).

events and the people involved were transformed by the legal process and by media coverage.

The wounded young man who committed this injury became a *criminal* and was thus dealt with as an abstraction, in stereotypes. The young woman who was injured became a *victim*, but her needs probably received relatively little attention. The events became a *crime*, and the *crime* was described and dealt with in symbolic and legal terms foreign to the people actually involved. The whole process was mystified and mythologized and thus became a useful tool in the service of the media and the political process.

"Crime" is prominent in media coverage. Studies have found that it is so in part because it sells. People are drawn to the sensational. But coverage is prominent also because it is "easy news." Unlike much other news, news about crime is simple to obtain. The reporter simply needs to stay in contact with the police and the prosecutor. But this "news" is often obtained uncritically. Crime news is often accepted from official sources without question and without independent verification. To maintain access to such news sources requires that reporters remain on good terms with police and prosecutor, and this does not encourage objectivity. Consequently, crime news is viewed through the eyes of the legal process and its professionals. Such news is not only one-sided but tends to encourage crime to be abstracted and mystified.

Crime is also an important tool for politicians. Crime can be an important beating stick. A position on crime is one crucial way to "position" oneself in our society. Are you tough-minded, realistic? Or are you soft, idealistic? A statement about crime is a way to take sides, as we saw in the 1988 U.S. presidential elections.

Again, however, the harms and events behind what we call crime get lost. The process is mystified, mythologized, until it is larger than—and distant from—life. In that process, we all become more fearful.

All of this has an impact on our sense of community. We have several options when faced with *crime*. We can draw together defensively, against the "enemy." A sense of community may be increased, but it is a defensive, exclusive, threatened community. Alternately, we can retire to fortified homes, becoming distrustful of others. The sense of community, already weak, becomes further eroded.

The issue of how we respond to wrongdoing, then, has important implications for our future.

PART II:

The Justice Paradigm

CHAPTER 5

Retributive Justice

Throughout the criminal justice process the wounds and needs of both the victim and the offender are neglected. Worse yet, injuries may be compounded.

Throughout this process, the phenomenon of crime becomes larger than life. Crime is mystified and mythologized, creating a symbol that is easily manipulated by politicians and the press.

Many have introduced attempts to reform this process over the past several centuries. The conclusion of some that "nothing works" or that no good has come of these reform efforts is inaccurate. Nevertheless, many if not most have gone astray. They have had all sorts of unintended consequences. Reform efforts have been used for purposes much different than originally envisioned. Prisons themselves were originally promoted as a humane alternative to corporal and capital punishment. Incarceration was to meet society's need for punishment and protection while encouraging reformation of offenders. Within a few years of their introduction, prisons became places of horror and the prison reform movement was born.

Recognition of the inadequacies and misuse of prison soon led to a search for "alternatives" to prison.[1] Numerous alternatives have been introduced, but their history has not been encouraging. Frequently they have served as alternatives to other "alternatives," not as alternatives to prison. Too often they have been alternatives to taking no formal action. Prison populations have continued to grow while "alternatives" expanded as well, increasing the total number of people under the control and supervision of the state. The "net" of control and intervention has widened, deepened, and lengthened, but without discernible effect on crime and without meeting essential needs of victim or offender.

Why is this true? Why are the actual needs of those involved in crime—whether transgressed or transgressor—so irrelevant in the "justice" process? Why are changes intended as reforms so often unsuccessful at altering this pattern? The answers lie in our shared understandings of what crime and justice are all about. Unless we address these fundamental definitions and assumptions, real change will be unlikely.

Are there in fact commonly shared assumptions about what crime and justice are all about? On the surface, we find considerable diversity, even among criminal justice professionals. Judges, for example, show tremendous variety in their perceptions about what outcomes are appropriate and why. This is a major reason behind the serious lack of uniformity in sentences. The diversity of philosophy and opinion has been highlighted by studies which have given judges

---

1. A considerable literature on the history and effects of "alternatives" has emerged. See, for example, David T. Rothman, *Conscience and Convenience: The Asylum and Its Alternatives in Progressive America* (Boston: Little, Brown, and Co., 1980) and M. Kay Harris, "Strategies, Values, and the Emerging Generation of Alternatives to Incarceration," *New York University Review of Law and Social Change*, XII, No. 1 (1983-84), pp. 141-170.

identical case histories, then asked them to indicate what their sentences would be. The range in outcomes is breathtaking. Each judge, each prosecutor, each probation officer operates according to his or her own understandings of what is appropriate, which can vary markedly.

So understandings of what should be done about crime vary. In the U.S., people frequently use the words *liberal* and *conservative* as a way of making sense of this diversity. We expect conservatives to demand quick, sure, and stiff punishment, to decry the rules which protect offenders' rights, and to emphasize offenders' choices to offend while downplaying their circumstances. We expect liberals to be more concerned with offenders' rights and circumstances. We assume that liberals and conservatives have quite different approaches to crime and justice.[2]

Yet the two "opposites" may not actually differ from each other very much. On closer analysis we find that most of us share assumptions and understandings which transcend liberal and conservative labels. Some of these assumptions are embodied in criminal law. Some are not. It is important to understand what they are.

When we identify something as a crime, a number of basic assumptions shape our responses. We assume that

1. Guilt must be fixed.
2. The guilty must get their "just deserts."

---

2. Liberal and conservative approaches are helpfully explored in Elliott Currie, *Confronting Crime: An American Dilemma* (New York: Pantheon Books, 1985). Cf. Nils Christie, "Crime, Pain, and Death" in *New Perspectives on Crime and Justice*, Issue No. 1 (Akron, Pennsylvania: Mennonite Central Committee, 1984).

3. Just deserts require the infliction of pain.
4. Justice is measured by the process.
5. The breaking of the law defines the offense.

Let's look at these assumptions in more detail.

Fixing Blame

The question of guilt is the hub of the entire criminal justice process. Establishing guilt is the central activity, and everything moves toward or flows from that event.

Since this event is so important, and the consequences so profound, elaborate rules govern this event. Once guilt has been established, concern about procedural safeguards and rights diminishes.

The centrality of guilt means that the actual outcome of the case receives less attention. Legal training concentrates on rules and processes related to guilt, and law students receive little training in sentence-negotiation or design. Consequently, few judges and even fewer lawyers have much training about appropriate outcomes of criminal cases.

Our preoccupation with blame-fixing means that we tend to be oriented toward the past. What happened? Who did it? These questions take precedence over what to do to solve the problems which the offense created (or out of which the offense arose). Legal professionals spend little time on what can be done to prevent a recurrence of future problems.

The concept of guilt which guides the justice process is a narrow, highly technical one which is primarily "objective" or descriptive in nature. Did the accused person commit the act as described by law? Did he or she intend to do it? Was the act contrary to law? Legal guilt asks simply whether the person charged in fact committed the act, and, if so, whether he or she is liable under the law.

In the legal system, offenses and questions of guilt are framed in terms much different from how the victim and the offender actually experience them. The legal charge may seem to bear little relationship to the actual offense, and the language of guilt and innocence may seem to have little connection to what actually happened. As several defenders of the system acknowledged recently, "legal guilt, not factual guilt . . . is the foundation of the criminal justice process."[3]

This is soon brought home to a defendant. He may be charged with something that sounds quite different from what he actually did. The charges may be the result of negotiation between his attorney and the prosecutor. Even if he committed an offense, he may not be legally guilty and may be advised to plead "not guilty." Thus he may come to believe that he is in fact not guilty. Even if he is legally guilty, his attorney will likely tell him to plead "not guilty" at some stage. In legal terms, "not guilty" is the way one says, " I want a trial," or "I need more time." All of this tends to obscure the experiential and moral reality of guilt and innocence.

Legally the question of guilt is an either-or question. Degrees of severity of the offense may vary, but in the end there are no degrees of guilt. One is guilty or not guilty. Someone must win and someone must lose. Nils Christie identifies the implications well: We view courts as teaching and upholding social norms, but in fact they teach the hidden message that people can be evaluated in simplistic dichotomies.[4]

---

3. Donald R. Ranish and David Shichor, "The Victim's Role in the Penal Process: Recent Developments in California," *Federal Probation*, XLIX, No. 1 (March 1985), p. 55.

4. Nils Christie, *Limits to Pain* (Oslo, Norway: Universitetsforlaget, 1981), p. 45.

Although the jurist's concept of guilt is technical and descriptive, an offender may have contact with professionals whose perspective is what theologian Tom Yoder Neufeld has called "prescriptive." This concept of guilt or responsibility concerns itself more with explaining why the offense happened, focusing on causality and predictability, usually in social and psychological terms.[5]

The psychologist, for instance, may approach the concept of guilt in terms that are neither legal nor moral. In fact, she may avoid the concept altogether. Rather, she will look at what psychological factors led to this event, perhaps viewing the behavior as evidence of illness or serious dysfunction. Meanwhile, the sociologist will focus on patterns and causes in terms of social forces in the family, the community, and the larger society. While the jurist will treat the offender as an autonomous individual making more-or-less conscious choices, social and behavioral scientists will view the offender at least in part as responding to a variety of larger forces. This perspective raises questions about the extent to which the offender is personally responsible, and perhaps about the extent to which he is an offender rather than a victim.

While specialists such as jurists and social scientists will consider the issue of guilt in their own ways, a third perspective will color most people's thinking—including many criminal justice officials. This concept is a more moralistic or "ascriptive" one. In the popular

---

5. This discussion of guilt draws heavily upon Tom Yoder Neufeld, *Guilt and Humanness: The Significance of Guilt for the Humanization of the Judicial-Correctional System* (Kingston, Ontario: Queen's Theological College, 1982). Cf. McHugh, *Christian Faith and Criminal Justice*, Chapter 7, and Patrick Kerans, *Punishment vs. Reconciliation: Retributive Justice and Social Justice in the Light of Social Ethics* (Kingston, Ontario: Queen's Theological College, 1982).

view, guilt is not merely a description of behavior but a statement of a moral quality. Guilt says something about the quality of the person who did this and has a "sticky," indelible quality. Guilt adheres to a person more or less permanently, with few known solvents. It often becomes a primary, definitional characteristic of a person. A person found guilty of theft becomes a thief, an offender. A person who spends time in prison becomes an ex-prisoner, an ex-offender, an ex-con. This becomes part of his or her identity and is difficult to remove.

The young offender in the case which I described earlier will forever be affected and defined by that offense, no matter what good qualities he has or may develop. The fact that he has offended will define his job possibilities, his career potential, the rest of his life. His guilt, not his other qualities, is likely to be decisive. Nothing in the criminal justice process will allow him to overcome that—not even if he repays his "debt to society" by serving his time.

The legal concept of guilt, then, is highly technical and removed from real-life experience. However, many concepts of guilt operate in a specific case which can be very confusing to an offender. His lawyer will talk to him about guilt in technical terms, and the process may encourage him to deny his guilt unless he is legally guilty or has no other choice. Meanwhile, he may see a psychological evaluator or therapist who will help him to understand his behavior in psychological terms, possibly muting his sense of personal responsibility. In addition, he may bump into a chaplain who will talk of moral guilt but also of mercy, grace, and forgiveness. This chaplain may suggest that his guilt is real, not merely technical, but that resolution is possible. Then there will be other people such as prison guards who reflect a popular concept of guilt which suggests that not only is his guilt real, but it is hard to get rid of. He is, in fact, "bad."

What does guilt actually mean? How can one who has offended make sense of it? Is he or she actually an offender or a victim? Is he really guilty? What is he guilty of? Is it possible to put it behind and start over? As Neufeld has pointed out, offenders are constantly confronted with the terminology of guilt, but denied the language and clarity of meaning to make sense of it. Moreover, mechanisms for resolution are lacking.

The legal and popular concepts of guilt which govern our responses to crime are confusing and even contradictory, but they have this in common: they are highly individualistic. Western law and values often are predicated on a belief in the individual as a free moral agent. If someone commits a crime, she has done so willfully. Punishment is thus deserved because it is freely chosen. Individuals are personally and individually accountable. Guilt is individual.

The basic assumption of human freedom and of personal accountability is important. Simple determinism is clearly inadequate. Still, there are problems with the forms our assumptions about freedom and responsibility take in Western culture.

Much evidence suggests that offenders often do not act freely or at least do not perceive themselves as capable of free action. As I suggested in the previous chapter, many people in our society do not see themselves as free agents, in charge of their own lives. Instead, they see themselves as shaped by almost irresistible forces—whether social-economic or providential. Ideas of human freedom and thus responsibility necessarily take on a different hue in such a context.

The atomistic understanding of guilt and responsibility also fails to take into account the context of behavior. Although each of us is responsible for the choices we make, the social and psychological context in which we find ourselves certainly influences our actual and potential choices. The social, economic, political, and psychological context of behavior is indeed important, but our individualistic concept of guilt ignores the context.

The motivation to do wrong is much more complex than our individualistic approach acknowledges. The apostle Paul certainly recognized the complexity of responsibility for wrongdoing. While he assumed that human beings make choices and are responsible for their behavior, he acknowledged that the simple image of a person as a totally free agent does not do justice to the pervasiveness and power of evil. In his letter to the Romans, chapter 7, Paul agonized over the power of evil in his own life, telling of his own tendency to do what he should not. And he suggested that there is a difference between actual and potential freedom, seeing freedom as a gift, not something intrinsic in an individual. Wrongdoing can be a pattern, shaped by a variety of forces, some of which are the result of choices and some which are not. Such patterns can be difficult to break.

With our individualistic concepts of guilt and freedom we assume that the individual is free to make choices and has anticipated the consequences of those choices. We assume that the person has modified his or her behavior to take this into account. This assumption ignores the question of whether individuals believe themselves to have this freedom. It assumes that they have the ability to anticipate long-range consequences. Furthermore, it expects them to make a connection between behavior and consequence. Moreover, it ignores the nature of wrongdoing as a complex pattern. Finally, it ignores the social, economic, and psychological context in which actions occur. Consequently, justice for offenders can be conducted without reference to social justice and without threatening the status quo. Punishment can be justly deserved, regardless of whether the social setting is just.

Perhaps this view of guilt and responsibility is inevitable in an individualistic, competitive culture which defines worth in terms of material and social success, and which defines success and failure in purely individual terms. Persons are judged in terms of their access to wealth and power. Those who fail to measure up are held individually responsible. They have not only lost: they are losers. The same is true for guilt. Guilt is defined as an individual failing. The context of an individual's behavior is ignored. Offenders have had various choices and, having accepted the wrong ones, are labeled as guilty.

To summarize, then, the fixing of blame is central to our understanding of justice. The administration of justice is a kind of theater in which issues of guilt and innocence predominate. The trial or guilty plea forms the dramatic center, with the sentence as a denouement. As a result, justice is preoccupied with the past to the detriment of the future.

The legal concept of guilt which guides the justice process is highly technical, abstracted from experience. This makes it easier for offenders to avoid accepting personal responsibility for their behavior. It also frustrates victims, who find it difficult to match the legal description of the event with their own experience. Both victim and offender are forced to speak the language of the "system," to define their reality in its terms instead of their own.

Because guilt is narrowly defined, centering on individual behavior, it allows us to ignore the social and economic roots and contexts of crime. We thus attempt to create justice by leaving out many of the relevant variables. And since guilt is viewed in either-or terms, it encourages a simplistic view of the world which tends to see things as good and bad, them and us. Justice becomes a drama of guilt, a morality play that allows us to make simple sense of the world.

But the legal concept of guilt operates alongside several other concepts. This fact in itself causes confusion for participants and may assist offenders in denying responsibility for action. Some of these assumptions—such as the indelible quality of guilt—have serious, long-term consequences for offenders.

Offenders need to be held accountable for what they have done. One dimension of accountability is understanding and taking ownership for wrongdoing. Our concepts of guilt, however, at best fail to encourage such accountability, and at worse make it more difficult. The lack of a process for resolving guilt encourages the use of "exculpatory strategies" such as rationalization and stereotypes as a way of shielding oneself from the heavy burden of this guilt. Alternately, offenders may be encouraged to fulfill the prophecy inherent in the label.

While the process focuses on questions of the defendant's guilt and responsibility, it tends to disperse responsibility for outcomes and to deny questions of collective responsibility for offenses. Key decision-makers (lawyers, prosecutors, judges, probation officers) are encouraged to see themselves as carrying out the law, doing their duty. They are encouraged to see that responsibility for the outcome of a case belongs to the "system." This means that those who "make" justice can deny personal responsibility for outcomes. They are also discouraged from acknowledging what they have in common with offenders as people.

Renate Mohr, in a paper on Canadian criminal law, has said it well:

How is it that we *do* punishing? It is done in a way that no single person can be held responsible for the deprivation of liberty of another person. The criminal justice system . . . was craftily designed as a series of discreet, self-contained compartments. He who lays the charge, he who bargains the charge, he who pronounces the sentence, and he who administers that sentence are all different people who have little or no contact with each other or the accused person. We have a special word for sealing the judge's compartment. Having completed their job of imposing the punishment, they become "functus." That means they need not, indeed ought not . . . concern themselves any further with the pains of the punishment they have imposed on another human being. And so the process ensures that violence may be done to others on a daily basis without any one person having to take responsibility.[6]

Just Deserts and Pain

Once guilt has been established, a second assumption comes into play. We assume that offenders must receive their "just deserts." Offenders must get what is coming to them. Justice must settle the score, "tit for tat." Crime creates a moral debt which must be repaid and justice is a process of righting the balance. It is as if there is a metaphysical balance in the universe that has been upset and that must be corrected.

This concept of justice tends to focus on abstractions rather than the harm done. It assumes that what is needed to settle the score in each case is knowable and attainable. And it assumes that what is needed to right the balance, to pay the debt, is punishment. Criminal justice officials see their job as meting out appropriate

---

6. Renate M. Mohr, "A Feminist's Analysis of the Objectives and Alternatives Re: Punishment," an unpublished paper presented to the Conference on Feminist Perspectives on Criminal Law Reform, Ottawa, Canada, 1987.

levels of punishment. Offenders are encouraged to believe that by taking their punishment, they are paying their debt to society.

On closer examination, offenders find it hard to feel they are actually "paying their debt" in this way. The "repayment" is terribly abstract, and there is no public resolution when the debt has been paid. The repayment does little good for the community. In fact, it actually costs the community money. To say to the offender, in effect, "You have harmed someone so we will even things up by harming you too," merely adds to the amount of harm in the world.

Guilt and punishment are the twin fulcrums of the justice system. People must suffer for the suffering they have caused. Only the infliction of pain will right the balance.

We must be honest in our use of language. When we speak about punishment, we are speaking about inflicting pain, intended as pain. Nils Christie has helped us to see that penal law is in fact "pain law" because it is an elaborate mechanism for administering "just" doses of pain.[7]

Usually we attempt to hide this reality. Ours is a culture which tries to avoid the reality of pain. We have tried to banish death from our consciousness so we give it over to professionals. We also call it by other names: we "pass away" rather than die.[8]

The unease with delivering pain is complicated by a taboo against revenge as a motive. This in turn heightens the need to deny the nature and motives of what we are doing.

We do not like pain and revenge, and certainly do

7. Christie, *Limits to Pain.*

8. Christie, *Crime, Pain and Death.*

not want to be thought of as inflicting it, so we hide and obscure it. Nevertheless, that is what we do when we do "justice." We inflict pain in response to crime.

So we give punishment over to professionals, to be carried out beyond our sight. We obscure its reality with a variety of rationales and terms. We talk of "correctional centers" rather than prisons and of "correctional officers" rather than guards.

We devise a variety of rationales for delivering pain. At some times we have done it in the name of treatment, as a means of rehabilitation. Often we do it to prevent crime, to deter this offender ("individual deterrence") as well as to discourage other potential offenders ("general deterrence") by the fear of similar consequences. We administer pain in the name of deterrence, in fact, in spite of substantial questions about whether such deterrence actually works. We administer pain in the name of deterrence in spite of questions about the morality of administering pain to one person for the purposes of *possibly* deterring another. We administer pain even though it may have little relevance to what the victim needs or to the problems involved in the offense. We administer pain, observes John Lampen of Northern Ireland, because we've been educated to believe that humiliation and suffering are what justice is about and that evil must be held in check by harshness rather than by love or understanding.[9]

Ironically, this focus on inflicting pain can interfere with the first focus, the establishment of guilt. Because of the threat of punishment, offenders are reluctant to admit the truth. Because the punitive consequences are

---

9. John Lampen, *Mending Hurts* (London, England: Quaker Home Service, 1987), pp. 61, 67ff.

so serious, elaborate safeguards of offenders' right are needed, and these can make it difficult to get at truth. Judges and jurors too may become less likely to convict when the potential punishment is seen as very severe.

The assumptions of just deserts and the imposition of pain mean that offenders are caught up in a tit-for-tat world. This in turn tends to confirm the outlook and life experiences of many offenders. Wrongs must be repaid by wrong and those who offend deserve vengeance. Many crimes are committed by people "punishing" their family, the neighbors, their acquaintances.

Studies of capital punishment have failed to find evidence that the death penalty deters. Some evidence shows that the example of the death penalty actually causes some people to kill.[10] Apparently the message some potential offenders receive is not that killing is wrong, but that those who wrong us deserve to die. The message that offenders must get their due, and that what they are due is punishment, may teach a lesson quite different than what we intend.

The threat to inflict pain on those who disobey has long been recognized as the basis of modern law. The essence of the state is often identified by political scientists as the "legitimate" monopoly on violence. As political philosopher J. W. Mohr has noted, the institutions and methods of law are thus part of the cycle of violence rather than a solution to it.[11]

10. For example, William J. Bowers and Glenn L. Pierce, "Deterrence or Brutalization: What Is the Effect of Executions?" *Crime and Delinquency*, 26, No. 4 (October 1980), pp. 453-484.

11. J. W. Mohr, "Causes of Violence: A Socio-Legal Perspective." Unpublished paper presented to the John Howard Society conference, "Violence in Contemporary Canadian Society," Ottawa, Canada, June 1986.

The Process

The primary goal of our justice process is the determination of guilt and, once that is determined, the infliction of pain. Following a direction set by ancient Roman law, however, justice is defined by the process more than by the outcome.[12] Procedure overshadows substance. Have the right rules and processes been followed? If so, justice was done.

The appeals process in the U.S. illustrates this well. Only in specialized circumstances can outcomes of trials be appealed on the basis of the outcome or on the basis of the facts. Rather, appeals usually center on whether correct procedures have been followed. An appeals court does not examine the original evidence in itself.

Several characteristics of this process need to be noted.

The process is adversarial. It assumes—and encourages—a conflict of interest between parties. Through the regulated conflict of opposing interests, the truth will eventually come out and the interests of the parties will be safeguarded. It assumes irreconcilable interests, and then goes a long way to ensure that they are. Adversarial justice tends to become a self-fulfilling prophecy.

Jerold Auerbach, in his history of dispute resolution in the U.S., has eloquently pointed out that this is also a supremely individualistic, competitive model. It not only grows out of, but helps to promote a fragmented, competitive society.[13]

---

12. On this and other issues, Herman Bianchi's work has been helpful. See, for instance, his unpublished manuscript, "Justice as Sanctuary."

13. Jerold S. Auerbach, *Justice Without Law?* (New York: Oxford University Press, 1983), pp. 138ff.

There are strengths to this model, but it is at heart a battle model, a regulated duel. It is no accident, therefore, that politicians and law enforcement so often use the language of "war on crime."

Liberals and conservatives in the U.S. may differ on where they put the emphasis, but both assume justice to be a conflict guided by rules. Conservatives, expressing what has been termed a "crime control" orientation, have tended to give more priority to fighting crime (note the language!) than to the rights of the accused. Liberals, on the other hand, have emphasized the centrality of individual rights—a "due process" model. Both, however, assume that justice involves a battle between hostile parties, regulated by rules.

In this emphasis on rules and process, priority is given to equity of treatment as a test of justice. The intention is that defendants be treated equally. Two characteristics of this emphasis on equity should be noted. First, the emphasis is more upon intent than upon actual outcome. In practice, even approximate equity in outcome is rarely achieved, as is illustrated by racial disparities in prison and death row populations. These outcomes are difficult to challenge, however, as long as one cannot show there was an intent to treat defendants inequitably.

Justice is imaged as a blindfolded goddess holding a balance. The focus is on equity of process, not of circumstances. The criminal justice process claims to ignore social, economic, and political differences, attempting to treat all offenders as if they were equal before the law. Since the process aims to treat unequals equally, existing social and political inequities are ignored and maintained. Paradoxically, justice may thus maintain inequities in the name of equity.

The justice process, ringed about as it must be with complex rules, requires dependence upon proxy professionals who represent offender and the state. This, in turn, removes the process of justice from the individuals and the communities which are affected. Victim and offender become bystanders, nonparticipants in their own cases. A huge bureaucracy with vested interests of its own is born. Our society's tendency to look to professionals to solve our problems is encouraged.

We tend, then, to define justice as procedures for a battle or game.[14] We emphasize the intent to treat people equally in the process, without regard to equity of circumstances and with less concern for equity of outcome. We find ourselves dependent upon proxy professionals in this complex process.

Crime as Lawbreaking

In our society, justice is defined as applying the law. Crime is defined as lawbreaking.

Instead of concentrating on the actual harm done or on what victim and offender have experienced, we focus on the act of breaking the law. The act of breaking a law, not the damage or conflict, defines the offense and triggers the justice process.

The emphasis on lawbreaking is what allows both the offense and guilt to be defined in purely legal terms. As I noted earlier, moral and social issues become not only secondary but often irrelevant. The context of the action is not considered except to the extent that it has legal implications. As Christie has rightly pointed out:

Training in law is training in simplifications. It is a trained incapacity to look at all values in a situation, and

---

14. Cf. John Griffiths, "Ideology in Criminal Procedure or a Third 'Model' of the Criminal Process," *The Yale Law Journal*, 79, No. 3 (January 1970), pp. 359-415.

instead to select only the legally relevant ones, that is, those defined by the high priests within the system to be the relevant ones.[15]

Social, moral, and personal factors are relevant only insofar as they are legally defined as relevant. Questions of social justice are rarely relevant. The "criminal act" is of decisive significance, and it is narrowly and technically defined.

Who Is the Victim?
I have tried to outline five assumptions that we make about crime and justice. We assume that

1. crime is essentially *lawbreaking;*
2. when a law is broken, justice involves establishing *guilt;*
3. so that *just deserts* can be meted out;
4. by inflicting *pain;*
5. through a *conflict* in which *rules* and intentions are placed above outcomes.

These assumptions and their implications help to explain some of our failures, but there remains still another essential element: our identification of the victim.

In criminal law, crime is defined as an offense against the state. The state, not the individual, is defined as victim. The state—and only the state—may respond.

Since the state is the victim, criminal law pits offenders against the state. In practice, this means one proxy professional representing the offender (defense attorney) is pitted against another professional representing the state (prosecutor), with still another professional (judge) acting as referee and arbiter.

---

15. Christie, *Limits to Pain*, p. 57.

Because the power of the state is so vast and civil liberties implications so profound, complex safeguards for the procedures are essential. Because the state is so impersonal and abstract, forgiveness and mercy are nearly impossible to achieve.

Since the state is defined as victim, it is not surprising that victims are so consistently left out of the process and that their needs and wishes are so little heeded. Why should their needs be recognized? They are not even part of the equation of crime. Victims are mere footnotes to the criminal justice process, legally necessary only if needed as witnesses.

Victim compensation and assistance programs have become popular in recent years. And indeed they should be. Nevertheless, they cannot be expected to have a major and lasting impact until we reexamine our definition of crime. As long as victims are not intrinsic elements in the definition of crime, we must expect them to be more pawns than participants.

The justice process does not seek reconciliation between victim and offender because the relationship between victim and offender is not seen as an important problem. Indeed, how could their feelings toward one another be taken seriously if both are not part of the equation?

The sixth assumption we make, therefore, is perhaps most important: that *the state is the real victim*. The implications of that assumption are profound.

Crime is an offense against the state. Justice consists of establishing blame and administering pain in a battle guided by rules. The process is assumed to be the responsibility—indeed, a monopoly—of the state.

Until we begin to question these assumptions, the changes we introduce may make little difference. Ours is essentially a retributive model of justice, and that model is at the root of many of our problems.

CHAPTER 6

Justice as Paradigm

During the past century we have become a bit more modest than we once were about what we know with certainty. We are less sure that what we think we know about the universe accurately portrays an objective reality outside of ourselves.

Historical and cross-cultural perspectives have helped us to see how much our view of the world is shaped by the particular lens through which we view it. Modern psychology has revealed hidden motivations for what we do and think, and has demonstrated that there are complex and overlapping layers of conscious and subconscious reality. As a result, we have to acknowledge that what we think we know as reality is often more complex and problematic than appears on the surface.

At one time the physical sciences seemed to promise certainty about the nature and structure of reality. In the late twentieth century, however, scientists are less confident that their pictures of reality actually mirror the physical universe. Many are also less insistent than they once were that their methods can be applied with equal value to all areas of reality. Although scientists were initially quite immodest, claiming certainty and promising answers, today the sciences tend to confirm certain limits to our understandings of reality. They are realizing that what they work with are models or "paradigms" rather than with photographic reproductions of reality.

The Importance of Paradigms

Prior to the seventeenth century, Western understandings of the world were governed by the Ptolemaic worldview. Everyone knew that the earth—and humankind—was at the center of the physical universe. The planets spun around this nucleus embedded in concentric glass globes. This image of the cosmos meshed with Aristotelian physics which explained motion in terms of purpose and the "nature" of things. Theology and physics thus supported each other.

People generally agreed that this worldview presented an accurate picture of the universe. Anything which did not fit into this perspective seemed nonsensical. As strange as this model may seem to us today, to the medieval and early-Renaissance mind it was common sense.

The seventeenth-century scientific revolution created a whole new picture of the world, and this perspective has shaped our understandings into the present age. The new framework, shaped by such pioneers as Copernicus and Newton, puts the sun at the center and recognizes the earth as one of the planets. This separates theology from physics. Newton's physics, which made this sun-centered cosmos seem workable, posits a rational, mechanistic universe which obeys knowable, rational laws. It assumes that regularities exist and that one can discover and quantify such phenomenon. It implies that one can explain such events in terms of cause-and-effect. Thus the past can be seen as a complete cause or explanation of the present. Moreover, the present shapes the future (but the future cannot shape the present).

The universe is therefore predictable, assuming that one can discover the correct factors. One basic rationality exists for the world, and with this rationality one can understand the world.

The Newtonian, "scientific" approach works well to explain and predict much of what happens in the visible, physical world. For years it was believed to represent an accurate picture of the structure of the world, applicable to the psychological as well as the physical world. It has formed our common sense.

Today we are learning, however, that there are definite limits to this understanding. These limits exist not only in areas such as psychology, but even in the physical world itself.

The Newtonian picture does work for bodies of "normal" size moving at "normal" speeds—the "see-and-touch world." However, scientists have found that when things get tiny or begin to move very fast, Newtonian science no longer works. Similarly, in the realm of genetics Newtonian assumptions often break down. In these situations, probability begins to take the place of "laws" and predictability. The future becomes hard to predict in cause-and-effect terms. In outer space at high velocity, "common-sense" concepts of time and space become inadequate as they become more plastic and intermixed. In this world, Einsteinian physics begins to take the place of Newtonian. One must begin to use a different picture of the world.

In *Einstein's Space and Van Gogh's Sky*, Lawrence Leshan and Henry Margenau, a physicist and a psychologist, have shown us that the traditional "scientific" worldview is also inadequate in art, psychology, and spirituality.[1] Here other dynamics are at work and we must use other ways of knowing. Human beings, for example, are able to project into the future and to shape their behavior accordingly. Here the future can indeed affect the present. Ideas of cause-and-effect must be tempered with the concept of purpose. Rational, mechanistic "laws" cannot be assumed. We must use other descriptions of reality.

The limits of traditional science in the domain of psychology are nicely captured in the "First Law of Animal Psychology."

> If an animal of known, stable genetic background is raised in a carefully controlled laboratory environment, and administered a precisely measured stimulus, the animal will act as it damn well pleases.[2]

Leshan and Margenau clarify and expand what philosophers of science have been saying for some time. Our definitions of reality in a particular culture and era are ways of constructing reality. They are in fact models, paradigms. They will "work" to explain and influence in some situations, but they may not in others. They are pictures of reality shaped by our particular needs and assumptions, and they may be quite incomplete.

Paradigms shape our approach not only to the physical but also to the social, psychological, and philosophical world. They provide the lens through which we understand phenomena. They determine how we

---

1. Lawrence Leshan and Henry Margenau, *Einstein's Space and Van Gogh's Sky: Physical Reality and Beyond* (New York: Collier Books, 1982). This represents a significant advance in paradigm theory. The present chapter owes much to their work.

2. Leshan and Margenau, *Einstein's Space,* p. 150.

solve problems. They shape what we "know" to be possible and impossible. Our paradigms form our common sense, and things which fall outside the paradigm seem absurd.

Our paradigms are particular ways of constructing reality, and our retributive understanding of justice is one such construct. The retributive paradigm of justice is one particular way of organizing reality. That paradigm shapes how we define problems and what we recognize as appropriate solutions. It is common sense.

However, it is in fact a paradigm. Like all paradigms, it has certain strengths. Like all paradigms, it is also a trap.

Christie has captured well the importance of paradigms in shaping our expectations:

> A warrior wears armor, a lover, flowers. They are equipped according to expectations of what is to happen, and their equipment increases chances that their expectations will prove right.

So also with the institution of penal law.[3]

Applying the Paradigm

Interestingly enough, we apply the retributive paradigm only in very limited situations. Many conflicts and harms occur every day, but most are handled informally or extralegally. Only a tiny minority ever enter the legal process. In other words, the legal system is only one of many ways to settle disputes and wrongs, and it is rarely used.

Of those few which do enter the legal system, however, most are channeled through civil law. In civil

---

3. Christie, "Images of Man in Modern Penal Law," *Contemporary Crises: Law, Crime and Social Policy*, 10, No. 1 (1986), 95.

procedures, person is pitted against person rather than against the state. The state plays the role of referee and arbiter. Whether or not to use the process is usually at the discretion of the people involved. And they can drop out of the process if and when they find a resolution.

Because the focus is on settlement rather than loss of liberty or life, civil procedures are less strictly regulated than criminal. For the same reason, the definition and criteria of guilt are looser. In fact, at stake are questions of liability and obligation rather than guilt, and degrees of responsibility are possible. Consequently, outcomes are less likely to be seen in dichotomous, win-lose terms than in criminal cases. Unlike criminal cases, civil cases usually result in some form of compensation.

Only a small fraction of disputes ever enter the specialized processes of criminal law. Once they do, however, a completely different set of assumptions and understandings takes over. Here the retributive paradigm reigns.

The proportion of disputes and harms which are "criminalizable" is quite small, then, and only a fraction of these are in fact "criminalized."[4] The selection of situations to define as criminal and then to actually process as criminal is actually quite variable and arbitrary.

Definitions of "crimes" vary through time and space, often in rather arbitrary ways. We define many harms

4. Louk H. C. Hulsman has argued this in a number of settings. See "Critical Criminology and the Concept of Crime," *Contemporary Crises: Law, Crime and Social Policy*, 10, No. 1 (1986), pp. 63-80. Cf. John R. Blad, Hans van Mastrigt and Niels A. Uildriks, eds., *The Criminal Justice System as a Social Problem: An Abolitionist Perspective* (Rotterdam, Netherlands: Erasmus University, 1987).

by individuals as crimes, for example, but ignore serious harms—often affecting many people—which are committed by corporations.

Of those acts which are "criminal," only a fraction become criminal cases. Again, the selection can be quite arbitrary. Factors such as status, race, and the ethnicity of the victim and offender play a part, for example. So do the priorities and workloads of prosecutor, the police, and the court system.

What is important is that we recognize what we call crime as the tip of a pyramid of harms and conflicts. Only some of those situations and behaviors are designated as potentially criminalizable. Only a smaller fraction are actually criminalized. We handle most of our wrongs and conflicts in different ways.

Once we decide to criminalize a certain event or behavior, we begin to define reality quite differently, in ways that may not correspond to the experience of the participants. The retributive paradigm creates its own reality. *Now* the offense is against the state, which determines the response. Punishment, not resolution or settlement, is seen as the appropriate outcome. Responsibility becomes absolute, defined in terms of guilt rather than liability. Outcomes are imposed with little participation by victim or offender. The retributive paradigm takes over, shaping our perceptions of what can and should be done.

Paradigms Change

Our understandings of what is possible and impossible are based on our constructions of reality. These constructs can and do change.

Thomas Kuhn, in an influential book entitled *The Structure of Scientific Revolutions*, has suggested that changes in scientific outlook come about through a series of paradigm shifts.[5]

One model or paradigm replaces another, thus causing a revolution in the way we view and understand the world. This pattern of changes suggests a possible pattern for paradigm changes in general.

The Ptolemaic paradigm, which shaped Western understandings until the seventeenth century, seemed to fit observed phenomena. If you lie on your back at night and use the north star as a point of reference, the stars and planets appear to be in a circular globe with the earth at the center. Also, they do appear to revolve. It made sense to think of the cosmos as a series of concentric "crystalline spheres" with the earth at the center.

The earth-centered universe fitted philosophic and theological assumptions as well. Humankind represented the pinnacle of God's creation and it was only logical that their dwelling would be at the center of the universe.

A number of phenomena did not fit this pattern. As telescopes were invented and the skies explored, this number grew. Comets seemed to move through the areas where glass globes were supposed to be, for example. Calculated distances seemed incorrect. And planets seemed to move backward at certain points in their orbit.

This latter phenomenon, called retrograde motion, was troubling, since it was difficult to see how this could happen if the planets were embedded in glass globes. Scientists decided that the planets must move in small orbits within the larger orbit. They called this phenomenon epicycles. As they observed more and

---

5. Thomas Kuhn, *The Structure of Scientific Revolutions* (Chicago: University of Chicago Press, 1970).

more retrograde motion, the number of epicycles grew phenomenally.

The dysfunctions in the Ptolemaic understanding multiplied in the early seventeenth century. At the same time, a series of new discoveries and theories emerged. Kepler published his "laws." Galileo suggested laws of motion. Through the lens of the telescope he developed, he began to observe the skies. Brahe began systematically to record movement in the heavens. Increasing numbers of phenomena simply did not fit the expectations of the paradigm.

Nevertheless, it was difficult to junk the Ptolemaic understanding. After all, it was common sense. It had been for centuries. And it was linked closely with many philosophic and theological understandings. To jettison this paradigm would be revolutionary and frightening. So scientists used a multitude of epicycles to patch it together and considerable pressure was put on the innovators to withdraw their claims.

By the early seventeenth century, however, more and more phenomena did not fit. At the same time, scientists were making new discoveries. Isaac Newton fit the pieces together in a paradigm that was so compelling, so sensible, that it could not be avoided. Newtonian physics allowed Copernicus' universe to work, making possible the new paradigm.

Kuhn suggests that by implication we can find in this scientific revolution a pattern for intellectual revolutions. He suggests that the way we understand phenomena is governed by a particular model, a particular paradigm. This governing paradigm seems to fit most phenomena and various exceptions are made for those phenomena which do not fit.

Over time dysfunctions begin to develop as more and more phenomena do not fit the paradigm. However, we keep trying to rescue the model by inventing epicycles, reforms, which piece it together. Eventually, though, the sense of dysfunction becomes so great that the model breaks down and is replaced by another. This cannot happen, however, before a new "physics" is developed. That is, a variety of building blocks must be in place before a new synthesis is possible and a new common sense emerges.

In an interesting article several years ago, Randy Barnett suggested that the history of our justice paradigm shows some of the symptoms of paradigm change.[6] As with the seventeenth-century scientific revolution, for example, the paradigm has long been recognized as having certain inadequacies and dysfunctions. A series of "epicycles" has been used to patch it together, but the sense of dysfunction is becoming too great to allow easy remedies.

In early applications of the retributive model punishment was severe. There were no safeguards against abuse and no relationship between the severity of the offense and the punishment inflicted. The idea of proportionate punishment was an Enlightenment invention which made punishment more rational and palatable. The idea was that if punishment can be made to fit the crime and thus be less arbitrary, less at the whim of those in authority, punishment would make more sense.

Prisons became popular as a way to apply proportionate punishment. Prison sentences can be measured in lengths of time and graded to fit the crime. They can be seen as scientific, logical. In an age when science and rationality were so important, proportionate pun-

---

6. Randy Barnett, "Restitution: A Paradigm of Criminal Justice" in *Perspectives on Crime Victims*, ed. Burt Galaway and Joe Hudson (St. Louis, Missouri: C. V. Mosby Co., 1981), pp. 245-261.

ishment was a sensible way to shore up the punishment paradigm. Prison terms became a way to apply the concept "scientifically."

Other epicycles have been constructed. Rehabilitation, for example, governed sentencing schemes during the first half of the twentieth century. It brought a new rationale for punishment. In the 1960s, however, rehabilitation was discredited and the discretionary, indeterminate sentences which were part of that "treatment" model were abandoned. That epicycle was replaced by the just deserts philosophy which underlies the mandatory and determinate sentencing laws popular today.

The search for alternatives to prison represents still another attempt to patch up the paradigm. Instead of seeking alternatives to punishment, the alternatives movement offers alternative *punishments*. By offering new ways to punish that are less expensive and more attractive than prison, proponents are able to prop up the paradigm. However, because it is only an epicycle, it does not question fundamental assumptions about punishment. It has thus failed to have impact on the very problems (e.g., prison crowding) which it was designed to address.

Community service orders have become a popular sanction, for example. When introduced they promised to take prison-bound offenders, relieving prison crowding. In actuality, they have usually provided a new form of punishing offenders who might not have been punished. Today electronic monitoring of offenders claims new possibilities for punishment and control.

Victim compensation and assistance may be viewed as another such epicycle. In the United States, proposals for such efforts tend to be based on claims of victims' rights. In England, arguments are more likely to focus on their needs and welfare. Both approaches seek to remedy a problem in the existing paradigm but neither questions basic assumptions about the state's and the victim's role in justice. They recognize a legitimate problem but not the root source of the problem.

The sense of dysfunction and crisis is widespread. At the same time, many people are groping for a new "physics" for understanding and responding to the situations we call crime. Perhaps the ground is being prepared for a shift in paradigm.

The source of many of our failures, I am arguing, lies in the lens through which we view crime and justice, and that lens is a particular construction of reality, a paradigm. It is not the only possible paradigm. In the following chapters, I will summarize some historical and biblical understandings. These suggest that our retributive paradigm is relatively recent and that other paradigms are conceivable. They also suggest some building blocks for an alternative vision.

PART III

Roots
and Signposts

CHAPTER 7

Community Justice: The Historical Alternative

Offenders have violated the state's laws. They must be punished. The state must take charge. All of this seems so natural and inevitable. Surely this retributive paradigm must have been with us for a long time. Surely it must represent a definite improvement over what went before. Surely it is what must be.

The retributive model of justice is not the only way we have envisioned justice in the West. In fact, other models of justice have predominated throughout most of our history. Only within the past several centuries has the retributive paradigm come to monopolize our vision.

Nor does the victory of this paradigm necessarily represent improvement. A common historical fallacy is to interpret history as progress. We view recent developments as almost inevitable improvements over the past. But the present is not inevitably inherent in the past nor does it always represent progress.

Historical interpretation has tended to focus on two developments in the history of "criminal justice": the rise of public justice at the expense of private justice, and an increasing dependence on prison as punishment. That both developments occurred in some form

is not in doubt. However, recent historical work raises
questions about the pattern and meaning of these developments.

Usually we think of the past as dominated by "private" justice. Private justice is characterized as private
vengeance, often uncontrolled and brutal. Modern public justice, in contrast, is controlled justice: more humane, more balanced, less punitive. We assume that
prisons are less punitive and more enlightened than
what went before. In this view, we have become more
civilized and rational in dispensing justice and punishment.

Reality is more complex than this conventional picture would imply. "Private" justice was not necessarily
private and did not necessarily involve vengeance.
"Private" settlements were not necessarily more punitive, less restrained, or less enlightened than state-
dispensed justice. On the contrary, public justice may
actually be more punitive in focus and may offer a narrower range of possible outcomes. Vengeance, while it
certainly could occur prior to state-based justice, was
only one of a much richer set of options. So-called private justice certainly had deficiencies, but the picture is
not as simple as we usually assume.[1]

---

1. In addition to works cited in this chapter, the following resources were
particularly helpful: George Calhoun, *The Growth of Criminal Law in Ancient
Greece* (Berkeley: University of California Press, 1927); Michael Ignatieff, *A
Just Measure of Pain: The Penitentiary in the Industrial Revolution, 1750-1850*
(New York: Pantheon Press, 1978); Stanley Cohen and Andrew Scull, eds.,
Social Control and the State, (New York: St. Martin's Press, 1983); John H.
Langbein, "The Historical Origins of the Sanction of Imprisonment for
Serious Crime," *Journal of Legal Studies*, 5, (1976); Langbein, *Prosecuting
Crime in the Renaissance, England, Germany and France* (Cambridge, Mas-
sachusetts: Harvard University Press, 1974); Alred Soman, "Deviance and
Criminal Justice in Western Europe, 1300-1800: An Essay in Structure,"
Criminal Justice History: An International Annual, I (1980), 3-28; Pieter
Spierenburg, *The Spectacle of Suffering: Executions and the Evolution of Repres-
sion* (Cambridge, England: Cambridge University Press, 1984).

Community Justice

The history of the West encompasses considerable diversity of structures and customs. Not surprisingly, local practices of justice varied in time and locale. Yet broad similarities existed in the overall understandings of what was involved in crime and justice in the pre-modern world. To some extent these similarities reflected common traditions. Greco-Roman and Germanic tribal culture, for example, shaped in part the medieval worldview. Shared experiences and needs also led to similarities in understandings.

Until well into the modern era, crime was viewed primarily in an interpersonal context. Most crime essentially represented a wrong toward or a conflict between people. As in "civil" conflicts, what mattered in the majority of offenses was the actual harm done, not the violation of laws or an abstract social or moral order. Such wrongs created obligations and liabilities which had to be made right in some way. The feud was one way of resolving such situations, but so was negotiation, restitution, and reconciliation. Victim and offender as well as kin and community played vital roles in this process.

Since crime created obligations, a typical outcome of the justice process was some sort of settlement. Restitution and compensation agreements were commonplace, even for offenses to the person. Laws and customs frequently specified a range of appropriate compensations for both property and personal offenses. These included formulas for converting personal injury to material compensation. Our concepts of guilt and punishment may represent a transformation (and a perversion, perhaps) of this principle of exchange. The Greek *pune* refers to an exchange of money for harm done and may be the origin of the word for *punishment*. Similarly, *guilt* may derive from the Anglo-Saxon *geldan* which, like the German word *Geld*, refers to payment.[2] Offenses created liabilities. Justice demanded some steps to make losses right.

The offender and the victim (or a representative of the victim in the case of murder) settled most disputes and wrongs—including those we call criminal—outside of courts. They did this within the context of their kin and community. Church and community leaders often played central roles in negotiating or arbitrating settlements, registering agreements once they were made. The administration of justice was primarily a mediating and negotiating process rather than a process of applying rules and imposing decisions.

Reflecting this understanding of the church's role, a French Reformed church elder in 1681 urged the church to "work diligently to reconcile any quarrels which may be known to members of the consistory."[3] Such quarrels included offenses we would call crime. The elders thus decided to make a list of conflicts, to urge disputants to settle, and to suspend from Eucharist those who did not come to agreement. The French "acts of accommodation" represented such agreements which were registered before a notary.[4]

As the preceding suggests, this approach to justice may be better termed community justice than private justice. Justice was private only in the sense that it was not state justice. Both the harm done and the resulting

---

2. J. W. Mohr, "Criminal Justice and Christian Responsibility: The Secularization of Criminal Law," unpublished paper presented to the Mennonite Central Committee Canada Annual Meeting, Abbotsford, British Columbia, January 22, 1981.

3. Soman, "Deviance and Criminal Justice," p. 18.

4. Bruce Lenman and Geoffrey Parker, "The State, the Community and the Criminal Law in Early Modern Europe," in *Crime and the Law: The Social History of Crime in Western Europe Since 1500*, eds. V. A. C. Gatrell, Bruce Lenman, Geoffrey Parker (London: Europa Publications, 1979), pp. 19ff.

"justice" process were clearly placed in a community context. Wrongs were often viewed collectively. When an individual was wronged, the family and community felt it as a wrong also. And family and community were involved in the resolution in substantial ways. They might generate pressure for a settlement or serve as arbiters and mediators. They might be called upon to witness or even help enforce agreements.

Community justice placed a high premium on negotiated, extrajudicial settlements, usually involving compensation. Nevertheless, two alternative approaches existed. Both tended to be choices of last resort, chosen either as a means of forcing negotiation or growing out of the failure of negotiation. Thus both represented a kind of failure, although their existence may have helped to ensure the working of the norm.

The Retributive Option

Vengeance represented one of these alternatives. This option was resorted to less often than is commonly thought for reasons that are obvious. Vengeance was dangerous. It often led to reciprocal violence and blood feuds. In societies characterized by small, close-knit communities, emphasis of necessity had to be on maintaining relationships. Here negotiation and compensation made much more sense than violence.

The possibility of vengeance certainly existed, but use of it was limited and its roles and meanings were often different from what we assume.

One limit on vengeance, which in turn confirms the importance of negotiated justice, was the existence of sanctuaries.[5] Throughout the medieval period until at

5. On sanctuaries see Herman Bianchi, "Justice as Sanctuary," unpublished manuscript; "An Exchange on Sanctuaries," *International Association for the History of Crime and Justice Newsletter*, November 1986, pp. 27-33; Michael R. Weisser, *Crime and Punishment in Early Modern Europe* (Atlantic

least the French Revolution, Western Europe was dotted with a variety of safe areas independent of other laws and authorities. Those who were accused of wrongdoing could run to these areas in order to escape private vengeance or even local authorities. Many of these were not long-term havens, but places of safety which allowed tempers to cool while negotiations went on. Some sanctuaries specified the length of time the accused could remain. But while there offenders were to be safe.

Dutch criminologist Herman Bianchi has suggested another possible role for such sanctuaries. He and his co-workers have found that pilgrims traveling to do penance stopped at such sanctuaries. These pilgrims appear to have been making their pilgrimage as a penance for a crime. This suggests that both penance and compensation may have been seen as appropriate responses to certain offenses.

While on a recent sabbatical leave in the English city of Winchester, I discovered the "House of Godbegot." This building, now a clothing store, is a remnant of the Manor of Godbegot which was bequeathed by Queen Emma in 1052 to the church. It was given complete rights to be self-governing, including the right of "excluding all other officers from the place." Surviving court records from the manor suggest that it served as a sanctuary for offenders until it was dissolved by Henry VIII in the 16th century.

Court records indicate that on several occasions people entered the sanctuary and apprehended offenders. But they also show that this was considered a violation of the sanctuary. A thirteenth-century statute in Win-

Highlands, New Jersey, Humanities Press, 1979), p. 54; Paul Rock, "Law, Order and Power in the Late Seventeenth- and Early Eighteenth-Century England," in *Social Control and the State*, eds. Cohen and Scull, pp. 191-221.

chester specified that one could not belong to both Winchester and the manor without paying a fine. The exception, significantly, was for those there "for felony." Both of these examples suggest the manor's role as a sanctuary for offenders.

Vengeance was also limited by a mixture of law and custom. For example, in medieval Europe the feud was not considered legitimate unless negotiations had been offered and refused. The well-known Old Testament formula, "an eye for an eye," was the kind of formulae which helped to regulate private vengeance throughout much of Western history.

"An eye for an eye" could of course be taken literally, and such vengeance could be brutal. However, in societies unregulated by formal legal codes and procedures, these formulae were not commands, but limitations on violence: "Do this much, but only this much." Responses were to be in proportion to the wrong and were not to escalate the conflict.

Moreover, persons have often understood these formulae as equations for determining compensation: "the value of an eye for the value of an eye." Settlements in money or property were quite common in our history, even in cases of serious violence. Such codes provided principles for determining compensation.

Even when "an eye for an eye" was taken literally, it was viewed as compensation. When someone dies or is hurt in a communally organized society, the balance of power between tribes, clans, or other groups is upset. Balance may need to be restored by evening out numbers. The formulaic violence was intended as much to balance power as to exact revenge.

Then as now, victims needed to be morally vindicated. They demanded public recognition that they had been wronged and public acknowledgment by offenders of their responsibility. Compensation was one way of achieving this vindication, but retribution sometimes provided a certain moral compensation as well. Sometimes also the threat of retribution served to encourage offenders to take such public responsibility.

The threat of retribution certainly existed, but it may have been a means as much as an end in itself. Moreover, the meaning and functions of retribution often reflected a compensatory vision. The system rested first of all on the necessity of compensating victims and repairing relationships. This usually necessitated negotiations toward a settlement which would acknowledge the offender's responsibility and liabilities.

Throughout most of our history there have been exceptions to this ideal of restitutive justice for certain kinds of crime. Early theocratic societies considered a limited number of offenses to have religious dimensions requiring special, "abnormal," responses. Certain sex offenses, for example, were especially heinous because they offended the deity. These brought collective guilt upon the whole society. In order to demonstrate their condemnation of such behavior and thus avoid sharing in the guilt, a symbolic cleansing was necessary. Such offenses were few and carefully proscribed by law and custom, however, and did not set the norm for most "criminal" offense.

In the early modern period in Europe a limited number of offenses were seen as a challenge to the moral and political order, thus requiring the application of violent responses. These included witchcraft, incest, sodomy, and certain types of particularly heinous homicides.

The Judicial Option

Vengeance was one alternative to the ideal of negotiated, restitutive justice. Appeal to established courts was another. Like vengeance, however, this option was usually a last resort when negotiations failed or in those situations where law or custom required it. It was chosen as a means of encouraging negotiated settlements. To the modern mind, members of this society were remarkably reluctant to use the formal machinery of justice.

During the Middle Ages in western continental Europe, for example, a variety of "official" courts existed. Some of these were state or royal courts. Others were operated by ecclesiastical, municipal, or seigneurial authorities. Even state courts, however, tended to operate within the context and principles of community justice.

Medieval courts were "accusatorial" in nature. Except in a few types of offenses (e.g., those against the person of the crown), even royal courts could not initiate prosecution without a request by the victim or the family of the victim. Without an accuser, there could be no case. There were no public prosecutors and few legal grounds for independent prosecution by the state except for an offense in which the crown itself was the actual victim.

Once someone initiated prosecution, the court's role was to see that the parties cooperated. It was to equalize power relationships insofar as it was possible, and generally to regulate the conflict. The courts thus served as a kind of referee. If the parties involved came to an agreement, they were free to terminate the case at any time. The state had no legal authority to continue prosecution without an accuser. Initiative was in the hands of those involved.

Persons usually turned to the courts only to pressure the other party to acknowledge responsibility and to settle. Extrajudicial forms of community justice were preferred well into the modern era. This reluctance to use the judicial option was based on a variety of factors. Preference for negotiated settlements was one. However, local resistance to the claims of central authorities was a major factor as well. So was the financial cost that prosecution could entail. Also, medieval courts often assumed a reciprocity of risk. If the accuser failed to make his case successfully, he might be subject to the consequences intended for the accused. An accuser would of necessity want to have a strong case before proceeding. Finally, royal courts often had the option of imposing a fine as an outcome. Since the money went to the authority operating the court, it did the victim little good.

The accusatorial model which shaped court structures and procedures thus operated in the context of community justice, which in turn placed a high premium on compensation and on participant initiative. Accusatorial courts confirmed the centrality of community justice.

An Assessment

Premodern justice is conventionally portrayed as vengeful and barbaric, in contrast to the more rational and humane approach of modern justice. Clearly that picture is too simplistic and too grim. Nevertheless, it would be equally wrong to wax nostalgic for a golden age which has been lost. Community justice had serious deficiencies. Methods for establishing guilt in contested cases were arbitrary and inaccurate, lacking safeguards. This form of justice worked most satisfactorily among equals. Where offenders were subordinate, justice could be summary and brutal.

Community justice could also put a heavy load on victims since the pursuing of cases depended upon their initiative and perhaps even their resources. Penalties for offenses considered especially heinous could be barbaric.

Yet negotiated, compensatory settlements which guided community justice represents an alternative understanding of crime and justice which is important. Traditional concepts of justice recognized that harm had been done to people, that the people involved had to be central to a resolution, and that reparation of harm was critical. Community justice placed a high premium on maintaining relationships, on reconciliation. Thus the paradigm of community justice may have reflected the reality of crime better than does our own, more "enlightened," paradigm.

Traditional justice is often characterized as punitive justice. Yet punishment was only one of many possible outcomes, and often represented a failure of the ideal. Community justice offered a wider range of outcomes than does our contemporary retributive paradigm. At minimum, we must revise our assessment of traditional justice to reflect its possibilities for retribution *and* reconciliation.

The Legal Revolution

No system of criminal law as we understand it existed in medieval Europe. No written body of law identified certain acts as crimes and prescribed certain punishments. Cases were not normally handled by legal professionals. Political and judicial authorities did have a recognized role, but it was quite limited. A variety of courts existed, but on the whole they functioned within the assumptions and parameters of community justice. They were used with considerable reluctance.

In the eleventh and twelfth centuries, however, a series of changes began which for the next several centuries lay the basis for a drastically new approach to crime and justice. These changes took centuries to mature and were fiercely resisted by many. The new model of justice was not victorious until the nineteenth century. Nevertheless, this metamorphosis, although protracted and often overlooked by historians, constituted what legal historian Harold J. Berman has termed a legal revolution.[6]

Earlier political authorities had felt constrained to shape "law" within the framework of customary understandings and practices. In the later medieval period they began to claim the right to make new law and to abrogate old. Formal, written law codes incorporating new principles began to replace custom. By the eighteenth and nineteenth centuries, a special body of codified law had been developed to cover certain harms and disputes called crimes.

New arguments and procedures began to open the possibility of state intervention and initiative in certain types of cases. On the European continent, prosecutors representing the state began to appear. In England justices of the peace came to represent the state in limited ways. Courts began to move from their reactive, umpiring role to claim ownership of certain types of cases. They began to take the initiative in beginning procedures and to compile evidence in such cases.

In continental Europe, the style of courts changed from accusatorial to inquisitorial. Here the court was responsible for bringing charges, compiling facts, and determining the outcome—often in secret. In England,

---

6. Harold J. Berman, *Law and Revolution: The Formation of the Western Legal Tradition* (Cambridge, Massachusetts: Harvard University Press, 1983) and "The Religious Foundations of Western Law," *The Catholic University of America Law Review*, 24, No. 3 (Spring, 1975), pp. 490-508. Berman's pioneering work is extremely important. Other important sources on early modern justice and the legal revolution are A. Esmein, *A History of Continental Criminal Procedures* (Boston: Little, Brown, and Co., 1913) and Weisser, *Crime and Punishment*.

an accusatorial framework was maintained due to the role of the jury and the retention of at least the form of private prosecution. Here too agents of the state took the place of citizens as the guiding force in "criminal" cases.

In such cases, the nature of the outcomes began to change. Punishment began to take precedence over settlements. Fines—which went to the state's coffers—began to replace restitution to victims. Torture came to be not simply an acceptable penalty but a forensic tool for finding truth. The actual victim's stake in all this decreased.

This process did not happen by a sudden, direct state takeover of large categories of cases. Instead, representatives of the state gradually insinuated themselves into the accusatorial process. Starting as an investigator, for instance, the state eventually became accuser. By 1498, French law recognized that the king or the king's procurator was a party to every action. Arguing first that it had a right to participate in cases, the state eventually claimed ownership.

State lawyers used a variety of legal devices and arguments, some new and some old, to justify state involvement. Accusatorial procedures had recognized that the "ordinary" way for cases to be initiated was by victims or their relatives. Some jurisdictions had left room for certain "extraordinary" prosecutions by the court or state in limited situations. In fourteenth-century France, for example, there were several ways that a court might take cognizance of an offense. The ordinary way was by accusation brought by accuser. However, in the case of "present misdeed" (if the offender was caught in the act) or by "common report" (when the offense and offender were commonly known) the court could intervene without a direct accuser. Also, some provision was made for initiating a case by "denunciation." Here there would be accusers, but they remained in the background, playing only a minimal role. As is so often the case, procedures intended as extraordinary in the long run became ordinary.[7]

The use of such legal devices was combined with new arguments. The crown began to claim that it was keeper of the peace. From that it was a short step to the claim that, when the peace was violated, the state was victim. That the role and claims of individual victims would be lost in this process is not surprising.

The Role of Canon Law

Not incidentally, the development of this new legal system with central authorities occurred within the context of an overall struggle for power. This struggle for hegemony occurred both *within* and *between* religious and secular structures. It profoundly affected the way justice came to be done. The development of canon law—the law of the Catholic Church—was a critical part of these struggles.

During the first Christian centuries, the church was decentralized. Gradually several competing power centers emerged, each claiming certain authority. Also, problems of internal discipline arose within the church. A primary concern of the papacy during the medieval years, therefore, was to consolidate its authority within the church. At the same time, the papacy was engaged in a struggle to claim authority equal to or above "secular" political authorities.

Centralizing secular authorities were beginning to emerge during this time, however, and with similar needs. They too needed to consolidate their power

---

7. See Esmein, *A History*, pp. 121ff.

within their realms by finding ways to subordinate other power centers, including the church.

Both religious and secular authorities, therefore, sought new arguments and devices which would help them consolidate their authority. Law from the late Roman Empire provided just such an instrument, first for the church, then for the state.

During the Republican era of Roman history, crime had remained primarily a private or community affair with the state having only a limited role. As the Empire emerged, however, a tradition of law developed which recognized an expanded role for the state in creating law and administering justice.

This law was largely lost after the sixth century, although it may not have been entirely forgotten. The rediscovery of Justinian's Code by the West in the late eleventh century may not have been an accident. Supporters of the pope and perhaps supporters of secular authorities as well may have been searching for some time. Once rediscovered in the eleventh century, Roman law created the basis for canon law, which became the fundamental law of the church. Later its outlines were adopted by secular powers throughout all of western continental Europe. It influenced English law to some extent as well.

Berman has examined this law and its adaptation. He notes that Roman law was a radical departure from customary practices. What was adopted was an autonomous body of law from a civilization remote in time and culture. This law introduced important new elements.

Roman law was formal, rational, codified law based on logic and fundamental principles. Instead of being based on custom and history, this law stood alone. Therefore, it provided central authorities with possibilities and methods for inventing new law and voiding old "laws." Also, Roman law assumed a central authority and thus provided a basis for "legitimate" initiation of action by central authority. Part of the attraction of Roman law, then, was the important role it gave to central authorities.

Roman law was written law, based on principles that were independent of specific customs. It had an accompanying method for testing and developing law (i.e., scholasticism). Roman law therefore could not only be systematized and expanded but could be studied and taught transnationally by professionals. This universal character helps explain its appeal and almost immediate spread to universities throughout most of western Europe.

From the base of Roman law, the church built the elaborate structure of canon law, the first modern legal system. This was a revolutionary development. It provided the papacy with an important weapon in its struggle for supremacy both within the church and in its relationship to secular political authorities.

By providing for prosecution by a central authority, it established a basis for attacking both heresy and clerical abuse within the church. The most extreme expression of this new approach was the Inquisition in which representatives of the pope ferreted out heretics and tortured them both to obtain evidence and to settle accounts.

No longer was the individual the primary victim. In the Inquisition, it was a whole moral order which was the victim, and the central authority was its guardian. Wrongs were no longer simple harms requiring redress. They were sins.

As this implies, canon law did not only represent the introduction of systematic, formal law and an enlarged role for central authorities. It implied a wholly different concept of crime and justice. Justice became a matter of applying rules, establishing guilt, and fixing penalties. Early Christian practice had focused on acceptance and forgiveness of wrongdoing, emphasizing the necessity of reconciliation and redemption.[8] Canon law and the parallel theology which developed began to identify crime as a collective wrong against a moral or metaphysical order. Crime was a sin, not just against a person but against God, and it was the church's business to purge the world of this transgression. From this it was a short step to the assumption that the social order is willed by God, that crime is also a sin against this social order. The church (and later the state) must therefore enforce that order. Not surprisingly, focus shifted from settlements between participants to punishment by established authorities.[9]

Canon law and its accompanying theology formalized concepts of free will and personal responsibility. This helped to lay a basis for a rationale of punishment. Imprisonment became a means of punishing wayward monastics, which led to the widespread use of imprisonment as punishment beginning in the eighteenth and nineteenth centuries.

Canon law introduced important new principles. These in turn were adopted and adapted by political authorities, serving as an important model for secular legal systems from England to Poland and Hungary.

---

8. Gerald Austin McHugh, *Christian Faith and Criminal Justice: Toward a Christian Response to Crime and Punishment* (New York: Paulist Press, 1978), pp. 14ff.

9. This kind of reasoning was not totally new, of course. The medieval trial by ordeal was based on related concepts. Medieval thought related behavior and nature. Because certain offenses were contrary to God and nature, nature could be expected to reject the criminal. An evil person tossed into water would float since the water, being pure, would reject him or her. An innocent person was expected to sink—a dubious victory if one could not swim.

The example of canon law is by no means a complete explanation for the development of a state-centered, retributive understanding of justice. England was less influenced by canon law than was the Continent. While it did not develop an inquisitorial justice system, nevertheless it did develop a system of criminal law with the state as a guiding force. Given trends in society and the needs of emerging nation states, justice may well have gone in a similar direction without the example of canon law. However, the pattern provided by this adaptation of Roman law did provide important techniques and concepts for use by political authorities in consolidating their positions.

The role of Christian theology in all this is uncertain. Some historians have argued that theological concepts of guilt and moral responsibility played a causative role, helping to create new concepts of crime, justice, and power which the state came to embody. Others have argued that the development of modern justice was based on the political needs of emerging nation states or on socioeconomic processes. Theology then followed, providing justification for these new forms. That there are links between theology and these developments is clear, however.

State Justice Victorious

Historians Bruce Lenman and Geoffrey Parker have suggested that Western history may be viewed as a dialectic between two basic models of law or justice: community and state.[10]

State justice reared its head early. Elements of it may be seen in the Babylonian Code of Hammurabi or in

---

10. Lenman and Parker, "The State, the Community and the Criminal Law." Lenman and Parker's thesis provides part of the framework for this chapter.

Solon's law reforms in ancient Greece. However, only in the past several centuries has true state justice become victorious, monopolizing our views about crime.

Community justice at its best represented negotiated, restitutive justice. Its sense is captured in *frith*, the Germanic tribal word for peace implying a horizontal, agreed-upon peace. State justice, however, is the "King's peace." It is vertical, hierarchical, imposed, punitive.[11]

While community and state justice may seem to be opposing concepts, it is more accurate to see them as poles on a continuum, with many variations in between.[12] On one pole is "pure" community justice involving negotiated settlements between the parties concerned. Justice becomes a bit more formal when other parties, perhaps appointed by political authorities, are involved as arbitrators or notaries. Accusatorial courts are even more formal, specifying a role for the state. At the end of the scale lies the true state court with state initiation, state discretion, state control, and the state as victim.

Community justice, as it operated in early modern Europe, contained elements of state justice. Perhaps the mix, the symbiotic relationship, between the two forms of justice allowed community justice to work. Perhaps the threat of state justice oiled the works of community justice. Perhaps the ability to choose arenas of settlement was important. As true state justice emerged victorious, however, understandings of what was appropriate and possible changed. Community justice was no

---

11. Bianchi, "Justice as Sanctuary," chapter 6, p. 13ff.

12. Cf. Herman Diederiks, "Patterns of Criminality and Law Enforcement During the Ancien Regime: The Dutch Case," in *Criminal Justice History: An International Annual*, I (1980), pp. 157-174.

longer an option for most events we call crimes.

By the end of the sixteenth century, the cornerstones of state justice were in place in Europe. New legal codes in France, Germany, and England enlarged the public dimensions of certain offenses and gave to the state a larger role. Criminal codes began to specify wrongs and to emphasize punishment. Some of these punishments were overwhelmingly severe, including torture and death. Economic sanctions also remained a possibility in many cases.

The sixteenth-century Protestant Reformation may have encouraged this trend toward punitive sanctions administered by the state. Luther actively endorsed the state as God's agent in administering punishment. Calvinism tended to emphasize images of God as a punitive judge. It also gave the state an important role in enforcing the moral order.

State justice represented the wave of the future, but it was not yet dominant and could not claim a monopoly. The eighteenth-century Enlightenment and French Revolution were required before state justice could make such a radical claim.[13] By the eighteenth century, the state had come to claim absolute power, which it exercised in exceedingly arbitrary and abusive ways. Almost unimaginable forms of torture and punishment were commonplace—not only for duly-convicted "criminals," but for suspects and political enemies. The crown claimed to be above the law, and the law was a crazy maze of custom and principle, logic and arbitrariness, special interests and public concerns.

---

13. In addition to sources cited previously, see Michael Ignatieff, "State, Civil Society, and Total Institutions: A Critique of Recent Social Histories of Punishment" in *Social Control and the State*. eds. Cohen and Scull, pp. 75-105; and Jacques Ellul, *The Theological Foundations of Law* (New York: Seabury Press, 1969).

The reformers of the Enlightenment sought to place law above governments, and to provide law with a rational foundation. Deeply critical of tradition and religion, which they saw as superstitious and illogical, they embraced a secular form of law based on natural law and rational principle.

In this process, Enlightenment thinkers began to formulate new conceptions of society and the state based on an implied social contract. Laws should reflect the will of larger society, they said, and governments should articulate and administer such laws. This is not to say that they saw ordinary people making political decisions. Most Enlightenment thinkers were decidedly not democrats! But they did begin to articulate a concept of government as representing the interests of society at large instead of special interest groups or the royal family.

Faced with the abuse of power by a state claiming to be absolute, eighteenth-century reformers could have attacked the assumptions of a centralized state. They did not. Instead, they not only assumed a powerful state but provided a basis for an enlarged power rooted in a new logic and a new accountability. The new logic consisted of a social contract and a new accountability to wider elements of the population and to law.

Cesare Beccaria's *On Crime and Punishment*, first published in 1764 and often cited as the foundation of modern penal law, was in part an expression of this Enlightenment approach. Beccaria assumed that law should be rationally rooted in the will of the entire community. He said it should be equally applied to all, and that it should be administered in a rational way *by the state*.

Beccaria posited that people decide their behavior on the basis of expectations about the pain and pleasure that will result from their choices. Law should administer rational and limited doses of pain, therefore, taking into account the amount of pain needed to outweigh the pleasure to be derived from the offense. The pain which is administered, however, should be proportionate to the wrong that has been done.

Beccaria's book provided a useful weapon with which to attack abuses by the state and traditional law. Rather than question the central role of the state in the business of justice, however, it provided a new legitimacy. Moreover, although understood by many as enshrining a fully rational, "utilitarian," concept of law, in fact it retained strong punitive and even retributionist elements.[14]

The French Revolution, which began in 1789 and extended into the next century, drew on Enlightenment roots but had a dynamic of its own. It too attacked custom and privilege, seeking to replace it with a rationalized concept of law and a new concept of the state. Like the Enlightenment, it embodied more, not less, ambitious concepts of power for the state.

The new criminal codes adopted by the revolutionary and Napoleonic governments illustrated these tendencies. They gave to the state strong prosecutorial powers. These codes were also quite punitive, but with a more rational and equitable focus.

Eighteenth- and early-nineteenth-century developments, therefore, were important in the formulation of the modern form of retributive justice. The state was provided with a new legitimacy as well as new mechanisms for exercising power. Law was given a new sanctity, making lawbreaking more reprehensible and

---

14. See David B. Young, "Let Us Content Ourselves with Praising the Work While Drawing the Veil Over Its Principles: Eighteenth-Century Reactions to Beccaria's *On Crime and Punishment*," *Justice Quarterly*, 1, No. 2 (June 1984), pp. 155-169.

consequences more "deserving."

Enlightenment thought and post-Enlightenment practice increased the tendency to define offenses in terms of lawbreaking rather than actual harms. To the extent that harms were important, emphasis was increasingly upon public rather than private dimensions. If the state represented the will and interests of the public, it was easier to justify defining the state as victim and giving up to the state a monopoly on intervention. Most importantly, the Enlightenment provided a new physics of pain.

Enlightenment and French Revolutionary thinkers did not question the idea that when wrongs occur, pain should be administered. Instead, they offered new justifications. They instituted more rational guidelines for administering pain. And they introduced new mechanisms for applying punishment.

The primary instrument for applying pain came to be the prison. The reasons for the introduction of imprisonment as a criminal sanction during this era are many. However, part of the attraction of prison was that one could grade terms according to the offense. Prisons made it possible to calibrate punishments in units of time, providing an appearance of rationality and even science in the application of pain.

Prisons also matched well with evolving sensibilities and needs. Publicity and physical suffering had characterized punishments during the Old Regime. Absolutist regimes had used brutal, public punishments as a way of making visible their power. New, more popularly based governments had less need for public displays of power as a basis for legitimacy. Moreover, people were becoming less comfortable with pain and death. Ways of handling death and illness changed, reflecting a need to hide or even deny these hard aspects of life.[15]

15. Spierenburg, *Spectacle of Suffering*, Chapter 6.

In that context, prisons provided a way to administer pain in private.

As the technology for imposing pain changed, so did the scope of what was intended. Early-modern forms of punishment punished the body, often in brutal ways. Modern uses of prison sought, as French historian Michael Foucault has noted, to reach the soul.[16] American Quakers who championed the prison[17] did so with the expectation of encouraging repentance and conversion. Later justifications claimed prisons as a laboratory for changing behaviors and thought patterns, for reshaping personality. A wonderful variety of reasons have been invented for using prisons to administer what Christie has called "pain with a purpose."

The roots of formal, state-centered justice go back many centuries, but state justice met considerable resistance. Only in the last century did it emerge victorious. The American experience is a case in point.[18] Portrayals of American justice often emphasize the early development of legal, public forms of justice, locating the origin of formal, public prosecution in the prerevolutionary period. Recent studies, however, have found that public prosecutors had only limited roles. They had little discretion to initiate or drop criminal

16. Michel Foucault, *Discipline and Punish: The Birth of the Prison* (New York, Pantheon Press, 1977). See also Ignatieff, *A Just Measure of Pain* and "State, Civil Society."

17. 1990 marks the two-hundredth anniversary of the first modern prison, the Walnut Street Jail.

18. See Josephine Gittler, "Expanding the Role of the Victim in a Criminal Action: An Overview of Issues and Problems," *Pepperdine Law Review*, 11, (1984), pp. 117-182; and Allen Steinburg, "From Private Prosecution to Plea Bargaining: Criminal Prosecution, the District Attorney, and American Legal History," *Crime and Delinquency*, 30, No. 4 (October 1984), pp. 568-592.

cases until the middle of the nineteenth century or even later. Instead, other forms of justice (including mediation, arbitration, and civil court procedures) were popular and persisted long after state justice was victorious. Restitution was a popular form of settlement, at least for property harms, and victims had important roles.

Eventually state justice was victorious. The establishment of public prosecutors with broad discretionary powers, combined with the spread of penitentiaries, were an important part of this process in the U.S. The result is that today, as Jerold Auerbach has so eloquently said, "Law is our national religion; lawyers constitute our priesthood; the courtroom is our cathedral, where contemporary passion plays are enacted."[19]

Dimensions of the Legal Revolution

The victory of state justice was long in coming. But as Berman has documented, it represented nothing less than a legal revolution of profound implications. The dimensions of this revolution in the way we do justice and think about justice may be summarized as follows.

First, at the core of this revolution was a movement from private or community justice to public justice. This movement began with the opening of possibilities for state-initiated prosecution. Eventually the state claimed partnership, then ownership, until finally, for harms and conflicts termed crimes, the state had a monopoly on justice.

In that process, the victim of crime was redefined, with the state becoming the legal victim. Victims were

19. Jerold S. Auerbach, *Justice Without Law?* (New York: Oxford University Press, 1983), p. 9.

abstracted and individuals became peripheral to the problem or the solution.

Second, concurrent with this process, justice came increasingly to be based on formal law rather than custom or convenience. Justice came to be equated with written law as interpreted and managed by professionals. Increasingly the test of justice was the process used.

Certain harms and conflicts came to be defined as different from others, activating criminal procedures in which the state was predominant. Others were left to civil law, where participants maintained considerable discretion and power.

Third, vengeance was one possible outcome of community justice. The state took over that option, decreasing the availability of other possibilities. Punishment became normative. Resolution and settlements became unusual and even illegal. Since punishment rather than restitution was normative, individual victims' standing in cases was reduced.

Interestingly, the church never mounted any serious criticism of this process. Concerned to control private vengeance and quick to acknowledge a role for the state, it provided active support.

As punishment became normal, new forms of punishment arose. Punishment also changed in symbolic meaning.

In the premodern world, the revenge motive clearly played a role when punishment was sought. At least as important to the idea of punishment, however, was vindication of the victim. Punishments were largely public. In imposing punishments, a symbolic statement of the moral rightness of the victim was implied.

In theocratic societies, punishment also involved a symbolic cleansing function that cleared the community of the pollution created by crime. Punishment demonstrated that society did not condone such actions, thus helping to maintain a sense of boundaries and self-identity for the community.

Newly-emerging governments were often highly personalized in the royal family and were concerned to secure their positions. Public, brutal punishment served as a symbol of the power of the state, a way of asserting and dramatizing its power. Justice in these circumstances was often no more than a theater of guilt and vindication which demonstrated the awesome power of central authorities.[20] That symbolic role helps to explain the severity of many punishments. They were meant to demonstrate the power of the state and the consequences of opposing it. Punishment had to strike terror. This role as symbol of state power also helps explain public resistance to some forms of punishment. The hangman was a particularly loathsome figure in many European communities, in part because he represented state-imposed justice.[21]

Today punishment is usually justified in pragmatic, utilitarian terms—as deterrence, as incapacitation, as rehabilitation. Behind it remain important symbolic functions, however, which may retain elements of earlier forms of punishment. As I observe punishment being imposed, I often suspect a need to dramatize the power of the state and the law over the individual.

Fourth, with changing concepts of justice came new understandings of crime and the criminal. Instead of an

20. Cf. Spierenburg, *Spectacle*, pp. 200ff.; Mark A. Sargent, review of Foucault in *New England Journal on Prison Law*, Spring, 1979, pp. 235-240; Heinz Steinert, "Beyond Crime and Punishment," *Contemporary Crises: Law, Crime and Social Policy*, 10, No. 1 (1986), p. 25; and Horace Bleackley and John Lofland, *State Executions Viewed Historically and Sociologically* (Montclair, New Jersey: Patterson Smith, 1977).

21. See Spierenburg, *The Spectacle of Suffering*, Chapter 2 and pp. 200ff.

individual wrong or conflict, certain behaviors became collective harms and social or moral heresies. Crimes were now a violation of both a social and supernatural order. The public dimensions were elevated above the private. This provided important justification for the state to enforce the social and moral order. Justice came to be seen as a righting of a balance, a metaphysical balancing of abstractions.

A Paradigm Shift

The legal revolution, as I have already suggested, involved a shift in paradigms, in ways of constructing and understanding reality. What underlay such a shift? A variety of answers can be and have been suggested.

Leshan and Margenau note that new paradigms emerge as an attempt to solve a society or culture's most pressing problems.[22] The scientific paradigm, they argue, emerged as an attempt to solve Western society's most desperate problem in the late Middle Ages. This was the problem focused by catastrophes such as the Black Death. Society was faced with a pressing need to control its environment, and therefore developed a paradigm adequate to do that. As other problems emerged, however, the paradigm was found to be inadequate, and new paradigms had to emerge.

What, then, was the problem which the retributive paradigm attempted to solve? Some explanations have centered on the growing complexity and anonymity of society as populations grew, as cities emerged, and as society became industrialized. Perhaps traditional methods of solving problems worked less well without a basis in community.

---

22. Lawrence Leshan and Henry Margenau, *Einstein's Space and Van Gogh's Sky: Physical Reality and Beyond* (New York: Collier Books, 1982).

Others have noted the need by society, or at least the upper levels of society, to control unrest. They have sought to reduce class conflict and to find ways to maintain order without disrupting patterns of social and political inequality.

A common interpretation points to the need to control private vengeance. In this view, vengeance was out of control, and only by giving the state a "legitimate monopoly on violence" could vengeance be controlled. Representatives of the state often advanced this argument. Historians have questioned, however, whether vengeance was as uncontrolled or the alternatives as limited as this explanation would suggest.

Part of the answer to our question may lie in the needs of emerging states to monopolize and exercise power. What was the problem which the retributive paradigm sought to solve? Perhaps it was the need of the state to legitimate and consolidate its power. The modern state is, in sociologist Lewis Coser's terms, a "greedy institution."[23]

At any rate, the paradigm shifted. But inadequacies in the new paradigm soon became apparent, and a variety of "epicycles" and modifications were introduced. Today the sense of dysfunction is high. Is another paradigm possible? If so, can it draw on elements of the past? Our tradition suggests some possibilities.

---

23. Lewis A. Coser, *Greedy Institutions* (New York: Free Press, 1974).

CHAPTER 8

Covenant Justice: The Biblical Alternative

Our past provides one model which demonstrates a different way: community justice. There is another model which to Christians is still more important: biblical justice.

That biblical justice should offer a sharp contrast to a retributive justice model may come as a shock. After all, the place in our society where the Bible seems to be cited most frequently is in just this arena. " 'An eye for an eye,' saith the Lord." What could be clearer than that the Bible mandates just deserts in the form of punishment for crime?

But there is more to "an eye for an eye" than meets the eye. On closer examination, this principle of "lex talionis" does not mean what most people take it to mean. Moreover, it most decidedly is not the overriding theme, the paradigm, of biblical justice.

What Does the Bible Say?

What does the Bible have to say about subjects such as crime and justice? Obviously it has many things to say. Not everything makes equal sense to us, given the age and situation we live in. Some passages even seem mutually contradictory on the surface.

Take, for example, the following examples of legal statements, all drawn from the Old Testament Torah.

If anyone injures his neighbor, whatever he has done must be done to him: fracture for fracture, eye for eye, tooth for tooth. As he has injured the other, so he is to be injured. (Lev. 24:19-20)

Do not seek revenge or bear a grudge against one of your people, but love your neighbor as yourself. I am the Lord. Keep my decrees. Do not mate different kinds of animals. Do not plant your field with two kinds of seed. Do not wear clothing woven of two kinds of material.
(Lev. 19:18-19)

If a man has a stubborn and rebellious son who does not obey his father and mother and will not listen to them when they discipline him, his father and mother shall take hold of him and bring him to the elders at the gate of his town. They shall say to the elders, "This son of ours is stubborn and rebellious. He will not obey us. He is a profligate and a drunkard." Then all the men of his town shall stone him to death. You must purge the evil from among you. All Israel will hear of it and be afraid.
(Deut. 21:18-21)

When he thus sins and becomes guilty, he must return what he has stolen or taken by extortion, or what was entrusted to him, or the lost property he found, or whatever it was he swore falsely about. He must make restitution in full, add a fifth of the value to it and give it all to the owner on the day he presents his guilt offering.
(Lev. 6:4-5)

Do not plow with an ox and a donkey yoked together. (Deut. 22:10)

Anyone who blasphemes the name of the Lord must be put to death. The entire assembly must stone him. Whether an alien or native-born, when he blasphemes the Name, he must be put to death. (Lev. 24:16)

Some passages seem to emphasize retribution. Others seem restorative. Some "make sense" to a twentieth-century mind. Others seem completely foreign or even barbaric. Obviously we cannot follow all of them. How do we choose which to use? How do we get an accurate picture?[1]

One approach which may reduce the number of interpretative problems is to limit ourselves to the New Testament, the most recent of biblical material. This method has merit since Christ himself made it clear that the "new covenant" superseded the old.

Clearly the New Testament must be our primary standard. But to ignore the Old Testament is to cut ourselves off from a wealth of material, much of which provided the background and roots of the New Testament. To understand more fully the dimensions of justice and of God's intent for humankind, we must take seriously the Old Testament. We cannot ignore the Old Testament if for no other reason that it is cited so often in our society.

When looking at the Bible, and especially the Old Testament, we must first remember that we are reading the literature from another world. This world is far from us not only in time and in geography but in philosophy, in political systems, and in social structure. As one would expect, laws took a much different form. They had much different purposes and were administered quite differently than in our own day.[2] Even un-

---

1. For discussions of approaches to biblical interpretation, see Willard M. Swartley, *Slavery, Sabbath, War, and Women: Case Issues in Biblical Interpretation* (Scottdale, Pennsylvania: Herald Press, 1983), Chapter 5; and Perry Yoder, *Toward Understanding the Bible* (Newton, Kansas: Faith and Life Press, 1978).

2. Helpful introductions to Old Testament law: Hans Jochen Boecker, *Law and the Administration of Justice in the Old Testament and Ancient East* (Minneapolis: Augsburg Publishing House, 1980); Dale Patrick, *Old Testament Law* (Atlanta: John Knox Press, 1985); Millard Lind's work, cited later.

derlying assumptions about subjects such as guilt and responsibility were different than ours, and this affected concepts of law and justice.

Guilt, for instance, was collective and so was responsibility. Because of this, certain types of crimes were felt to contaminate the entire society. To relieve such guilt, collective, ceremonial expiation was necessary and the responses suggested in the Old Testament for certain offenses thus have a sacrificial character that seems foreign to us.

All of this may make the law codes in Leviticus or Deuteronomy look rather strange to us. As the preceding selection suggests, topics of concern which to us seem appropriate in a legal code, such as murder and theft, are mixed in with topics that do not (e.g., regulations about agriculture, food, clothing, marriage, worship). Some offenses and responses clearly have religious and cultic dimensions while others appear more straightforward.

Because our worlds are so different, it can be quite problematic to apply biblical—particularly Old Testament—legal and judicial prescriptions to our own situations. Certainly it is not adequate simply to pick a law selectively and to "plug it in" to our own situation. Nor is it accurate to take isolated concepts and to graft them on to other philosophic bases. As we shall see, that approach has in fact led to a perversion of important biblical ideas. Rather, we must attempt to understand underlying principles and intentions, then to move from them to concepts such as law and justice. As Christ suggested, we must grasp the spirit, not just the letter, of the law. Only after that can we begin to understand individual biblical "laws" to make contemporary applications.

These basic perspectives and directions are what we must try to unravel here. This is not the place for a detailed analysis of the function, form, content, and administration of Hebrew law. My approach, rather, will be to sketch what appear to be underlying directions, then to look at concepts of justice and law given those directions. Finally, I will try to draw some conclusions about the meaning of crime and justice which have application today.

Two foundational concepts are essential if we are to begin to unravel biblical thinking about law and justice (or, for that matter, anything else): shalom and covenant. It is here that we must start.

Shalom: A Unifying Vision

An essential theme of the biblical message, expressed in both the Old and New Testaments, resides in the Hebrew word *shalom*. (In New Testament Greek, the comparable word is *eirene*.) Shalom is not a peripheral theme, nor is it simply one among many themes. Shalom is a basic "core belief" around which many other important beliefs are organized. Shalom encapsulates God's basic intention, God's vision, for humankind. Consequently, we must understand salvation, atonement, forgiveness, and justice from their roots in shalom.

The usual translation of shalom, "peace," captures one aspect of the concept, but does not adequately convey all the connotations of the word. Shalom refers to a condition of "all rightness," of things being as they should be, in various dimensions. Old Testament scholar Perry Yoder's authoritative study found that shalom, as used in the Bible, has three basic dimensions of meaning.[3]

---

3. Perry B. Yoder, *Shalom: The Bible's Word for Salvation, Justice, and Peace* (Newton, Kansas: Faith and Life Press, 1987). This chapter draws heavily upon Yoder's discussion of shalom, justice, law, and covenant.

Contrary to common assumptions, shalom usually refers to material or physical conditions or circumstances. God's intent is for humanity to live in physical well-being. At minimum this means a situation where things are all right. At some points, however, it seems to point to more, to prosperity and abundance. At any rate, the visions of the future, articulated so graphically by the prophets, include health and material prosperity and an absence of physical threats such as illness, poverty, and war.

A second dimension of shalom has to do with social relationships. God intends for people to live in right relationship with one another and with God. To live in shalom means that people live in peace, without enmity (but not necessarily without conflict!).

The Bible makes it clear that this includes living in just economic and political relationship with one another. Over and over the Bible makes it clear that oppression and injustice are contrary to shalom, that they do not represent right relationships, that they must not be allowed to exist. Shalom depends on right relationships between people, and this means the removal of oppression. Marked divisions in material conditions and in power which result in the impoverishment and oppression of some cannot coexist with shalom, for shalom means the well-being of all in a society. When that is lacking, shalom cannot exist.

A third application or dimension of shalom in its biblical use applies to the moral or ethical realm. According to Yoder, shalom here refers to a "straightforwardness." The concept functions in two ways in this application. It refers to honesty or absence of deceit in dealing with one another, and to a condition of blamelessness (i.e., being without guilt or fault). Shalom involves a condition of honesty, of moral integrity. This dimension of shalom, while important, is the one mentioned least often in the Bible.

Shalom defines how God intends things to be. God intends people to live in a condition of "all rightness" in the material world; in interpersonal, social, and political relationships; and in personal character. There can be no shalom when things are not as they ought, and the absence of shalom is at the heart of the criticisms the Old Testament prophets leveled at God's people. The vision of shalom also shapes hopes and promises for the future.

While the fuller implications of shalom are beyond our scope here, this vision of shalom underlies the meaning of other central pillars of biblical faith. The shalom vision also helps us understand God's actions and God's promises throughout the biblical story.

The shalom theme undergirds Old Testament thought, but it is also central in the New Testament. New Testament writers used *eirene* like shalom to define God's good news for humanity.[4] Like shalom, *eirene* refers to peace between people and God and between people themselves on a variety of levels.

Christ's life, teaching, and death show a pattern for such living. They transform divine-human relationships but they also transform relationships between people. In Yoder's words, "Jesus came so that things might be as they ought to be both among people and between people and God and even in nature."[5]

Thus reconciliation is an important theme in the New Testament, but the state of "all rightness" which God intends continues to have the material and physical dimensions that it had in the Old Testament.

---

4. Yoder, *Shalom*, pp. 19-21.

5. Yoder, *Shalom*, p. 21.

Covenant: Basis for Shalom

The basis and primary model of shalom in the Bible is the concept of covenant.[6] Part of what differentiated the Israelites so sharply from their contemporaries in the ancient Near East was the belief that God had made a covenant with people. This concept of covenant profoundly shaped concepts of law, of justice, of social order, of faith, of hope. Laws which were similar to—and perhaps in some cases borrowed from—those of surrounding societies were radically transformed by this covenant.

In the biblical milieu, a covenant was a binding agreement made between two parties. Covenants assumed a personal relationship between parties and implied certain reciprocal responsibilities and commitments. Biblical faith assumes a covenant between God and people, a covenant based on God's righteous acts of salvation. The central act of salvation in the Old Testament was an act of liberation, the Exodus from Egypt. This act of salvation was performed because of God's love, not because it was earned or deserved.

Although the Exodus was definitional, the Old Testament story is one of repeated deliverance, repeated acts of salvation. The prophets understood these repeated acts of deliverance to be part of God's commitment stated in God's covenant to God's people. Even though God's people frequently fell down on their end of the responsibilities implied in the covenant, the

---

6. In addition to Yoder's work (e.g., pp. 75-82), I have depended heavily upon Millard Lind's discussions of covenant and law. See "Law in the Old Testament" in *The Bible and Law*, ed. Willard M. Swartley, Occasional Papers No. 3 of the Council of Mennonite Seminaries (Elkhart, Indiana: Institute of Mennonite Studies, 1983); and *The Transformation of Justice: From Moses to Jesus*, Issue No. 5 of "New Perspectives on Crime and Justice: Occasional Papers" (Akron, Pennsylvania: Mennonite Central Committee, 1986).

prophets maintained that God had remained faithful to the original promise.

The people occasionally renewed their covenant with God and the result created conditions for shalom since the relationship was now right. Covenant, therefore, provided both the basis for and a model of shalom.

But a covenant implies mutual responsibilities. Concepts of law and justice provided ways for people to understand or work toward shalom by heeding these responsibilities.

In the Old Testament, the fundamental act of liberation which provided the paradigm of covenant and the basis for the shalom vision was the Exodus from slavery in Egypt. The new act of liberation represented by the life, death, and resurrection of Christ formed the basis for a "new" covenant, a new way of living together. The New Testament, perhaps better understood as the new covenant, grew out of previous understandings and continues the concepts of shalom and covenant, but in a renewed form. A new day in relationships between God and humanity—and between persons—has been born. However, as in the Old Testament, the basis for this covenant is God's act of salvation and liberation. This act by God provides us a way of living together in shalom that involves mutual responsibilities between God and people and among people.

The covenant of the Old Testament was based on a central act of salvation and liberation. This covenant created the basis for a new society, one which would be different than others, with operating principles of its own, and which would work toward shalom. The covenant of the New Testament too is based on a foundational act of salvation and liberation. It likewise creates the basis for a new community, with its own operating principles, and which will provide the basis for God's work of shalom in this world. Covenant continues to be foundational.

Shalom and Covenant as Transforming Forces

Shalom and covenant were transforming forces in the development of ideas of law and justice in biblical society. As it developed, Hebrew society encountered many of the same needs and pressures as did other ancient Near Eastern societies. Like the Babylonian ruler Hammurabi, for instance, Hebrew leadership faced the need to standardize and unify in the face of growth, urbanization, and specialization. Legal and judicial tools used in this process sometimes had common forms or even common roots in Israel and in other Near Eastern kingdoms. However, Hebrew ideas of law and justice were radically different in substance from those of Hammurabi. They were different because they were transformed by shalom and covenant.

Old Testament scholar Millard Lind has written that Hammurabi's law was state law. It was hierarchical, imposed, punitive, rooted clearly in a distant and all-powerful king.[7] Hebrew law, on the other hand, assumed that God was the source of all authority, above even kings. This God was personal, faithful, and concerned about the underdog and about the human condition generally. These qualities were embedded in the vision of shalom and the belief in covenant. Taken together, they transformed justice and law. As a result, covenant justice stood in marked contrast to state law.

The concept of transformation is important, but has another dimension as well. God works within the limits of an age, within the limits of understanding and vi-

---

7. Lind, *Transformation of Justice,* p. 3.

sion. Human understandings are always incomplete and, as Christ reminds us (Mark 10:5), allowances are made for this. Yet God pushes the limits, seeking to expand our understandings and insights. Consequently, human understandings continued to develop throughout the biblical story, throughout history. As part of this process, Christ built upon, but often transformed, old covenant understandings. Concepts of shalom and covenant were transforming forces, shaping ideas of law and justice, but they in turn were transformed as well.

The concept of transformation, therefore, makes sense in several dimensions. Lind has helpfully termed this multidimensional process "the transformation of justice from Moses to Jesus."

Covenant Justice

As the shalom concept implies, the question of justice is not marginal to the Bible. Justice is not an "elective" we can choose to ignore.[8] Justice has to do with shalom relationships and thus is fundamental to what God is about, to who God is, and to what we are to be. In fact, justice serves as a measuring stick to test for shalom!

It is no surprise, then, that the topic of justice recurs frequently in the Bible. Nor should we be surprised that when the prophets condemned Israel for straying from their God, they made it clear that injustice was the problem as much as failure to worship as they ought.

No single Hebrew word directly translates as "justice," but two words often translated into English in

---

8. In addition to works cited, see Matthew Fox, *A Spirituality Named Compassion and the Healing of the Global Village, Humpty Dumpty and Us* (Minneapolis: Winston Press, 1979).

this way are "sedeqah" and "mishpat."[9] Neither carries with it quite what we mean in English by justice, but both have to do with righteousness, "right-ordering," with making things right. To do justice is to make things right, and the history of God's covenant relationship with Israel is a model, a promise, and a call. The norm for justice, then, arises from Yahweh's relationship with Israel. Biblical justice is rooted in a vision of shalom, modeled by God's definitional acts of salvation in God's covenant relationship with God's people. The way God responds to wrongdoing provides an important window into God's justice.

What then are the qualities of God's justice?

Following Greek and Roman cues, we tend to divide justice into areas such as "social justice," sometimes called "distributive justice," and "criminal justice" or "retributive justice." When we talk about wrongs having to do with the distribution of wealth and power, we call these questions of social justice. When we talk about wrongs legally defined as crimes we categorize this as the realm of retributive justice.

Distributive justice we understand to be difficult to obtain, a distant goal. In the meantime, however, we actively pursue retributive justice. We assume, that is, that one can separate the areas of justice and deal with them in different ways.

Biblical justice is more holistic. It sees both spheres as part of the same whole. Injustice of any kind, in any sphere, is contrary to shalom. The acts of the one who oppresses are as serious as those of the one who assaults or robs. Both are contrary to shalom. Justice is not separable.

---

9. For example, in Micah 6:1-8. See Lind, *Transformation*, p. 1. See also note 12.

Our fields of retributive and distributive justice, though governed by different operating rules, both assume that justice has to do with the fair distribution of rewards. Both have to do with seeing that people get what they deserve. Thus both retributive and distributive justice are based on the principle of reciprocity, of just deserts. This often suggests a kind of abstract, moral order where imbalances must be righted. It also implies that justice must be deserved or earned. Distributive justice, for example, assumes that on some level people have to earn what they get. Likewise, a central concern of retributive justice is making sure people receive the punishment they deserve.

The Bible recognizes some place for this "tit-for-tat" justice, but its emphasis is elsewhere. Tit-for-tat justice must be tempered by shalom justice, and shalom justice, like God's salvation, concerns itself with need, not merit.

The ultimate rejection of legalistic, tit-for-tat justice appears throughout the biblical story. It appears in the many places where consequences mandated or recognized in the law are not carried out. Although Cain may have deserved the death penalty for committing murder, God rejects this penalty. When Hosea's wife commits a capital sin, she is spared. The woman who had committed adultery deserved to die by contemporary standards. However, Jesus rejects the penalty. This rejection of just deserts is demonstrated also in Christ's story of the workers in the vineyard. Workers who began at noon are paid the same generous amount as those who began in the morning, contrary to the expectations of tit-for-tat justice.

Above all, this rejection of just deserts is demonstrated by God's own actions, actions designed to model shalom justice. Confronted by repeated wrongdoing, God did not give up on Israel.

We tend to assume that love and mercy are different from or opposite to justice. A judge pronounces a sentence. Then as an act of mercy, she may mitigate the penalty. Biblical justice, however, grows out of love. Such justice is in fact an act of love which seeks to make things right. Love and justice are not opposites, nor are they in conflict. Instead, love provides for a justice which seeks first to make right.

It is worth noting here that Western concepts of romantic and emotional love complicate our understanding of love as a source for action. Biblical concepts of love do not rule out how we feel. Certainly Christ makes it clear that feelings of hate are as serious as actions. Yet love is not defined as a mushy emotion. Love is, rather, a conscious act of looking after the good of another. When the Bible talks of love, the words usually connote action and volition more than feelings.

Biblical justice seeks to make things right, and the emphasis is upon liberation. God seeks to make things right by liberating those who are oppressed materially, socially, and emotionally. Justice is an act of liberation. This liberation does not happen because it is merited but because it is needed.

Our image of justice, borrowed from the Romans but put in legal form by the French Revolution, is of a blindfolded woman neutrally balancing a scales. Justice is treating people as equals, without partiality. But is it really just to treat unequals equally? Does this not perpetuate inequality? Biblical justice seeks to make things right, and this often means liberation for the unequal. Thus biblical justice shows a clear partiality toward those who are oppressed and impoverished. It is clearly on the side of the poor, recognizing their needs and disadvantages. Biblical justice is open-eyed, with hands outstretched to those in need.

Since biblical justice seeks to make things better, justice is not designed to maintain the status quo. Indeed, its intent is to shake up the status quo, to improve, to move toward shalom. The move toward shalom is not necessarily good news to everyone. In fact, it is downright bad news to the oppressor. This too stands in contrast to that justice which—by working to maintian "order"—works in fact to maintain the present order, the status quo, even when it is unjust.

The test of justice in the biblical view is not whether the right rules are applied in the right way. Justice is tested by the outcome. The tree is tested by its fruit.[10] It is the substance, not the procedure, that defines justice. And how should things come out? The litmus test is how the poor and oppressed are affected.

The actual administration of justice in biblical times, although necessarily an imperfect reflection of this ideal, nevertheless often embodied the assumptions of covenant justice.[11] When wrongs were done, ordinary people went to the city gates to seek justice in a "legal assembly" in which citizens participated. The focus of this court, sometimes called an "organization of reconciliation," was not to satisfy some abstract concept of justice but to find a solution. The word for judgment here can be translated *settlement*. Restitution and compensation were common outcomes. The passage from Leviticus 6 quoted earlier in this chapter was characteristic in that it called for replacement of loss, plus addi-

---

10. Cf. Herman Bianchi, *A Biblical Vision of Justice*, Issue No. 2 of *New Perspectives on Crime and Justice: Occasional Papers* (Akron, Pennsylvania: Mennonite Central Committee, 1984), p. 7.

11. See Boecker, *Law and the Administration of Justice*, pp. 31ff.

tional compensation. In Exodus 18, Moses established a system of judges. His aim was not to identify winners and losers but to ensure that "all these people [would] go home satisfied" (i.e., in shalom; v. 23).

Given this emphasis, it should be no surprise that the words for paying back (*shillum*) and for recompense (*shillem*) have the same root word as shalom. Restitution was a way of seeking to make things right. Recompense, sometimes translated *retribution* but implying satisfaction rather than revenge, provided vindication. Both had to do with restoring shalom.[12]

Offenses were understood to be wrongs against people and against shalom, and the justice process involved a process of settlement. This is the model in Micah 6. The people of Israel had violated God's intent, violating covenant. God's grievances are stated in a form which was probably characteristic of contemporary lawsuits. Through the prophet Micah, God's grievances—and the consequences of such wrongs—are presented in graphic form. Then comes the ultimate out-

---

12. See Dan W. Van Ness, *Crime and Its Victims* (Downers Grove, Illinois: InterVarsity Press, 1986), p. 120; and Van Ness, "Pursing a Restorative Vision of Justice," in *Justice: The Restorative Vision*, Issue No. 7 of *New Perspectives on Crime and Justice: Occasional Papers* (Akron, Pennsylvania: Mennonite Central Committee, 1989), p. 18.

Millard Lind has suggested the following definitions:

Shillum: Requital, retribution, reward (Hosea 9:7; Micah 7:3).

Shillem: Recompense (Deut. 32:35).

Shalom: That well-being which arises out of the covenant relationship.

Mishpat: The social expression of God's righteousness; the norm for behavior which arises out of the divine-human relationships, and the interhuman relationships based thereupon.

Sedeqah: As a synonym of *mishpat*, it may be translated *justice*. Where it differs, *mishpat* may refer to applied justice, while *sedeqah* is an attribute of God's character as sovereign leader. Often it may be translated *salvation* or *victory*. When used of humans, it may refer to moral conduct, those human acts which are a remembrance of Yahweh's deeds and teaching.

Eirene: Harmony and concord between nations and individuals; security and well-being which arises out of the covenant relationship (see shalom).

come. In spite of this, God will not give up. Micah 7:18 demonstrates God's justice: "Who is a God like thee, who pardons iniquity and passes over the rebellious act. . . . He does not retain his anger for ever, because he delights in unchanging love."

As this example suggests, retribution is one theme in the Old Testament. Usually, however, punishment by God appeared in the context of shalom. Punishment was not—as it usually is for us—the end of justice. It was often aimed at restoration or at breaking the power of the oppressor (i.e., at "vindicating" the oppressed). And this shalom context served to limit its retributive potential.

Likewise, punishment was often understood to occur in a context of love and community. That is, punishment was accompanied by renewal of the covenant. This meant that punishment could be viewed as fair, as deserved. It also kept open the possibility of eventual reconciliation and restoration rather than perpetual alienation. It was thus restorative rather than destructive. Punishment was not the end. The concept of shalom thus tempered the operation of retributive justice.

Biblical justice decidedly was not a forensic inquiry into wrongdoing to establish guilt and decide what punishment was merited. Rather, biblical justice was an attempt to right wrongs, to find solutions that would bring about well-being.

Covenant Law

The focus of biblical justice was on substance much more than legality. Wrongdoing was not defined primarily as nonconformity to rules, to laws. Justice was not the right application of rules.

This may seem somewhat problematic to us. We tend to see in laws the safeguard of both justice and order. We therefore see offending as breaking the law and we see justice as applying the law. The Bible does neither.

The Ten Commandments, the most famous (though not necessarily the most characteristic) of biblical laws, provide one window into the nature and function of law. We tend to interpret such law from the perspective of our own law so we see them primarily as imperatives, prohibitions: "You must do this or else." But this collection of laws can be read in the future indicative. The Ten Commandments, like much biblical law, are like invitations, promises: "If you are really living as you should be, this is what life will be like. You will not kill. You will not steal. . . ." The Ten Commandments—and indeed the whole Torah—are intended as a pattern for living in covenant, in shalom.[13]

The Torah is thus a pattern for living in shalom under the old covenant. We misunderstand if we see it primarily as a set of imperatives, of rules that must not be broken. It is a promise, an invitation, an example of what life should be like.

If the Torah offers a pattern for living in community under the old covenant, the Sermon on the Mount provides a pattern for living under the new covenant. Again, we misread this set of teachings if we see it primarily as rules, as imperatives and prohibitions. Like the Torah, it is an invitation, a pattern for shalom. Both are less rules than a glimpse of what life will be like when we are really living, when we live in shalom.

Biblical law is thus intended to provide a direction: "This is the direction in which you should move." *Torah* translates *teaching* and may include both story and directive or "halaka," the way to walk. Given our understanding of the rigidity and finality of law, we are

---

13. Herman Bianchi, *A Biblical Vision*, pp. 5-7. See also his discussion of *Torah* and of *sedeqah* here.

often amazed at the way the Israelites questioned and debated the law. But laws were to be used in teaching moral principle. Moreover, they were starting points for discussion, for people were supposed to talk about the law. Martin Buber, in his German translation of the Bible, perhaps captures best the spirit of biblical law when he calls them "wise indications." They set a direction and in doing so establish principles, but they are meant to be discussed.

Biblical law was intended as a means, not an end in itself. The best law was unwritten law, and it was the spirit, not the letter, of the law that mattered. This was the original focus of the Torah, but in time it became rigidified. And it was this legalism, this rigidity, that Christ so objected to. This perspective also helps to explain why so often the spirit, not the letter, of the law that seems to be carried out in the Old Testament. As Christ pointed out in his comments about the Sabbath, law was made for people, not people for the law. The intent was that "wise indications" be internalized, that the thrust of the law be followed.

The Bible contains many detailed statements of law on a wide variety of topics. We tend to understand these laws from the perspective of our own laws, so we interpret them as codes. In fact, however, many of these represent past judicial decisions, offered as a guideline for finding principles which might apply in other situations. Again, they are wise indications more than rules for conduct. They provided principles for use in settling disputes, not bases for establishing guilt and meting out punishment.

Law was intended as a means, not an end. It was an instrument for building shalom, for building relationships that are all right. Its characteristic purpose was not to punish but to redeem, to make things right.

The law codes of ancient Israel's contemporaries

combined elements of community law and state law.[14] Ultimately, however, laws such as Hammurabi's code, like today's law codes, were impersonal and based on the coercive power of the state. The covenant basis of biblical law, however, meant that obedience was to be in response to God's liberating acts, not to governmental coercion. Moreover, both law and political authorities were subject to God. Neither had independent standing. Law was not autonomous, and neither the formulation nor the administration of law was to be centered in the state. Although Israel adopted a form of kingship, laws were never reoriented to center on this, so the administration of law remained primarily a matter for local courts and clan.

The form of biblical law reflects its basis in covenant and its focus on redemption. Biblical law commonly begins by a statement of what God has done, then moves to proper response. That is, statements of law often begin with what is known as the "motive clause." God has performed an act of liberation salvation, *therefore* this is the proper response. The Deuteronomic law on slaves, for example, is coupled with this motive clause.

> You shall remember that you were a slave in the land of Egypt, and the Lord your God redeemed you; therefore I command you this today.

Similarly, the Ten Commandments follow a reminder of God's act of liberation (Deut. 5:15). This motive clause is characteristic of much Old Testament law,[15]

---

14. This discussion of law draws primarily from Lind, Yoder, Boecker, and Patrick. However, see also John E. Toews, "Some Theses Toward a Theology of Law in the New Testament" in *The Bible and Law*, ed. Willard M. Swartley, pp. 43-64.

15. See especially Deuteronomy 12-28 and Leviticus 17-26. For short discussions of the motive-clause pattern, see Lind, "Law in the Old Testament," pp. 17ff. and Yoder, *Shalom*, pp. 71ff.

but the same "therefore" pattern is used by Paul in the New Testament.

The motive clause, the "therefore" pattern, is directly rooted in the covenant concept and in this form the law itself became a restatement of covenant. The law is based on God's acts of saving liberation, performed out of love and not because they are deserved. Since God has done this for us, here is how we should respond. The pattern, then, is grace followed by law. The form of the law states not only our responsibility but the reasons for it: God's redemptive acts.

The real story of the Bible, from the Old Testament into the New, is this: God does not give up. It is precisely in this way that we are to imitate God, to be "perfect": in indiscriminate love, in love that is undeserved, in forgiveness, in mercy.

The phrase "an eye for an eye" is commonly taken to summarize the retributive "tit-for-tat" nature of biblical law. However, the phrase only occurs three times in the Old Testament. In the New Testament, Christ specifically rejects it. "You have heard it said, 'an eye for an eye,' " he says, "but I tell, do good to those who harm you." Was he in fact directly contradicting Old Testament law?

"An eye for an eye" was a law of proportion intended to limit rather than encourage revenge. It limited destructive vengeance. In fact, this legal principle laid the basis for restitution, providing a principle of proportionality in response to wrongdoing.

So the focus of "an eye for an eye" was not on retribution but on limit and proportion. But there is more. In the covenant context, with its focus on liberation, this common principle also established equity.

Leviticus 24 is one of three places where this phrase occurs. The "eye for an eye" principle is poetically stated in several versions. Immediately following this appears the admonition that there must be one standard for all, for the stranger as well as the native. Strangers were often the dispossessed, the oppressed. God frequently reminded the people of Israel that they were once strangers, that it was God's own act of salvation that rescued them. In turn, they should take care of the stranger among them. A guidepost like "an eye for an eye," then, established the idea that all should be treated alike.

The motive for vengeance exists and is recognized in the Old Testament, but biblical law early sought to establish limits. One such limit was the "lex talionis," the guideline of proportionality.[16] Another were the cities of refuge. Deuteronomy 19 mandates the establishment of sanctuaries where those who committed unintentional homicide could run and be safe while feelings cooled and negotiations were conducted.

The Biblical Paradigm

All of this suggests that the paradigm of biblical justice, including Old Testament justice, is not to be found in retribution. The key is not in "an eye for an eye" but in the motive clause. God's own response to wrongdoing is normative.

When confronted by wrongdoing, God is described in human terms as being angry, full of wrath. The roots of words translated *wrath* and *anger* (*aph, anaph, naqam*) have graphic connotations including heat, snorting, and

---

16. See Patrick, *Old Testament Law*, chapter 4; Roland de Vaux, *Ancient Israel* (New York, McGraw-Hill, 1961), p. 149; Boecker, *Law*, 171ff.

deep breathing. God becomes angry and is sometimes understood to punish.[17]

Here again, however, we must be careful in translation. Students of Hebrew report that several root words often translated retribution and punishment may mean to restrain, to teach, to make right. The concept of punishment may be present, but often with different connotations than that of our English word.[18] Moreover, Paul reminds us in Romans 12:19, quoting the Scriptures, that such punishment is God's business, not ours.

These connotations help to make sense of what seems to be a contradiction between the descriptions of God as punisher and God as slow to anger and overflowing in loving kindness (e.g., Exod. 34:6; Num. 14:18). God punishes, but God is also faithful. Israel repeatedly does wrong, and God becomes angry, but God does not give up. God moves, in other words, through wrath to restoration. That retribution is subordinate to shalom tempers and limits retributive justice.[19]

---

17. See Virginia Mackey, *Punishment in the Scripture and Tradition of Judaism, Christianity and Islam,* a published paper presented to the National Religious Leaders Consultation on Criminal Justice, convened by the National Council on Crime and Delinquency in Clarement, California, in September, 1981, p. 43. See also C. F. D. Moule, "Punishment and Retribution: An Attempt to Delimit Their Scope in New Testament Thought," *Svensk Exegetisk Arssbok,* XXX (1966), pp. 21-36; James E. Lindsey, Jr., "Vengeance," in The Interpreter's Dictionary of the Bible, supplementary volume (Abingdon: Nashville, 1976), pp. 932-933. On God's wrath, Mort MacCallum-Paterson's writing has been most helpful. See, for example, "Blood Cries: Lament, Wrath and the Mercy of God," *Touchstone,* May 1987, 14-25; and *Toward a Justice That Heals: The Church's Response to Crime* (Toronto: United Church Publishing House, 1988).

18. Bianchi, *A Biblical Vision,* pp. 1-2. Cf. Moule, "Punishment and Retribution."

19. Yoder, *Shalom,* p. 36.

This character of God's justice is demonstrated dramatically in passages such as Leviticus 26 and Deuteronomy 4. The people of Israel receive graphic descriptions of the horrible consequences of wrongdoing. Terrible things will happen. Yet the passages end by promising that God will not give up. God will not destroy them. God is faithful and compassionate.

In the New Testament, Christ's focus is even more clearly on restorative responses to wrongdoing. This presents no radical break from the Old Testament direction, no rejection of the overall thrust of the old covenant. Rather, it provides an unfolding of understanding, a continued transformation of justice.

The Bible begins with the story of a murder. The Bible recognizes here that unlimited retaliation is a normal, human response. Genesis 4 portrays the "law of Lamech" as seventy times seven, almost without end.[20]

But soon revenge is limited. In the case of Cain, the first story of a murder, the "normal" response of death is not applied. And in Leviticus we find "an eye for an eye," the principle of limit, of proportionality.

Included is still another limit: love your neighbor. Do not take vengeance on your brother or sister. Vern Redekop has provided a helpful translation of Leviticus 19:17-18.

Do not let your mind be filled with hatred toward your brother or sister. Confront your associate, making a strong case to him or her. Don't let yourself get carried away with a wrong course of action (sin). Do not take vengeance and don't maintain angry feelings against the

---

20. Clarence Jordan has outlined in several places this movement from unlimited retaliation to unlimited love. See, e.g., *Sermon on the Mount* (Valley Forge, Pennsylvania: Judson Press, 1973), rev. ed., pp. 63ff.

people in your community. Love your neighbor as yourself. I am your Lord.[21]

Shalom is possible only if we look out for the welfare of one another, even in wrongdoing.

Christ continues this theme, deepening and broaden-
ing its application. The story of the good Samaritan
points out that our neighbor is not simply one of our
own kind. We have responsibilities beyond our own
people. We are, in fact, to do good even to those who
harm us. Not unlimited retaliation, the law of Lamech.
Not limited retaliation, the law of talion. Instead, unlimited love. It is no accident, perhaps, that he extends
this to seventy times seven, a number almost beyond
imagination. From unlimited retaliation to unlimited
love—we have come full circle.

The God who saves, freeing from oppression regardless of merit, is limited in wrath but unlimited in love
(in the poetic language of Deuteronomy, "to a thou-
sand generation"). It is God's unlimited love, not God's
wrath, which we are told to imitate. The motive clause
is also a model clause.[22]

The motive clause, not "lex talionis," captures the
essence of covenant justice. Restoration, not retribution, is the paradigm.

In chapter 2, I sketched a number of assumptions on
which our present "retributive" model of justice is
based. How then do these measure up to a biblical
"yardstick"? The following chart compares biblical and
contemporary assumptions about justice.

---

21. Church Council on Justice and Corrections (Canada). "Update"
(Spring 1985).

22. Lind, *Transformation*, pp. 5ff.

Concepts of Justice, Biblical and Modern

Contemporary Justice	Biblical Justice
1. Justice divided into areas, each with different rules	1. Justice seen as integrated whole
2. Administration of justice as an inquiry into guilt	2. Administration of justice as a search for solutions
3. Justice tested by rules, procedures	3. Justice defined by outcome, substance
4. Focus on infliction of pain	4. Focus on making right
5. Punishment as an end	5. Punishment in context of redemption, shalom
6. Rewards based on just deserts, "deserved"	6. Justice based on need, undeserved
7. Justice opposed to mercy	7. Justice based on mercy and love
8. Justice neutral, claiming to treat all equally	8. Justice both fair and partial
9. Justice as maintenance of the status quo	9. Justice as active, progressive, seeking to transform status quo
10. Focus on guilt and abstract principles	10. Focus on harm done

11. Wrong as a violation of rules	11. Wrong as violation of people, relationships, shalom
12. Guilt as unforgivable	12. Guilt forgivable though an obligation exists
13. Differentiation between "offenders" and others	13. Recognition that we are offenders
14. Individual solely responsible; social and political contexts unimportant	14. Individual responsibility, but in holistic context
15. Action as free choice	15. Action as choice, but with recognition of the power of evil
16. Law as prohibition	16. Law as "wise indicator," teacher, point for discussion
17. Focus on letter of law	17. Spirit of law as most important
18. The state as victim	18. People, shalom, as victim
19. Justice serves to divide	19. Justice aims at bringing together

Our system of justice is above all a system for making decisions about guilt. Consequently, it focuses on the past. Biblical justice seeks first to solve problems, to find solutions, to make things right, looking toward the future.

Today's justice seeks to administer to each his or her just deserts, to make sure that people get what they "deserve." Biblical justice responds on the basis of need, often returning good for evil. Biblical justice responds because shalom is lacking, not because justice is deserved.

Our first—and often only—response after guilt has been established is to deliver pain as punishment. Once delivered, the process of justice has ended. When punishment occurs in covenant justice, however, it is not usually the end but the means toward ultimate restoration. Moreover, punishment is primarily God's business. The primary focus of biblical justice is to make things right, to build shalom, by acting in aid of those in need.

Today the test of justice often is whether the proper procedures have been followed. Biblical or "sedeqah" justice is measured by the substance, by the outcome, by its fruits. Does the outcome work to make things right? Are things being made right for the poor and the least powerful, the least "deserving"? Biblical justice focuses on right relationships, not right rules.

Our legal system defines offenses as violations of rules, of laws. We define the state as the victim. In biblical terms, however, wrongdoing is not a contravention of rules but a violation of right relationships. People and relationships, not rules or governments or even a moral order, are the victims.

The assumptions of biblical justice are thus quite different than our own. But a biblical critique of modern justice goes beyond the assumptions I outlined in chapter 2. Biblical justice does not allow us to divorce questions of "crime" from questions of poverty and power. Justice is a whole. It cannot be fragmented. Corporations which commit fraud or which harm people through destruction of the environment are as responsible for their actions as are those individuals who commit murder. Moreover, the social context of crime must be considered. One cannot separate criminal acts

or actors from the social situation which lies behind
them. Unjust laws of whatever kind must be challenged.

Contemporary justice seeks to be neutral and impar-
tial. It seeks to treat people equally. It sees as its primary focus the maintenance of order. Because of this,
and because it can separate questions of criminal justice from social justice, the order which it tends to
maintain is the present order, the status quo. All too
often, therefore, modern law is a conservative force.
Biblical justice, on the other hand, is an active, progressive force seeking to transform the present order
toward one which is more just. In doing so, it looks
out especially for the poor and the weak.

Contemporary justice puts the state and its coercive
power at the center, as source, guardian, and enforcer
of law. Biblical justice puts people and relationships at
the center, subjecting both law and government to
God.

Biblical justice, then, provides an alternate paradigm
that critically challenges our own state-centered, retributive approach.

A Historical Short-Circuit

Contrary to common assumptions, then, biblical justice is primarily restorative rather than retributive. If
this is true, how did such a misconception develop?
How was the restorative theme overwhelmed by the
retributive?

Some have argued that such misconceptions developed as the result of a "historical short circuit" arising
from the mix of biblical with Greco-Roman ideas.[23]
Concepts such as the law of talion, which had a specif-

___

23. E.g. Herman Bianchi, "Justice as Sanctuary."

ic meaning in the context of covenant and shalom, were taken from their context and grafted onto a more punitive and abstract Greco-Roman philosophy. Ideas of retribution and penalty lost their grounding in shalom and became ends in themselves apart from any restorative context or purpose. Greco-Roman interests in abstract principles and ideals led to an abstraction of concepts of justice and just deserts which were contrary to the spirit of biblical law. Thus the original focus was lost and perverted while some of the old forms were retained. Consequently, the new hybrid perspectives appeared to have biblical roots.

With that done, people began to look back at the Bible through this lens, interpreting and translating passages from that perspective. Working from a retributive mind-set which emphasized rigid laws, guilt, punishment, and condemnation, it was easy to find in the Bible such themes. It was also then easy to overlook the larger, more important, story of restoration.

Our understanding of a central biblical event, the atonement, may be a case in point. Perry Yoder explains that the Bible itself offers no developed theory of atonement (i.e., of Christ's death).[24] Rather, it offers a series of images, metaphors, and insights which theologians have used to construct various explanations.

A central question for many people has been why Christ died, why one person's death could "atone" for the sins of others. The theories which developed in answer to this question tend to interpret the rest of the Bible from the viewpoint of Roman ideas of justice.

Some atonement theories, for instance, see God as an angry judge who needs to be appeased. People are guilty sinners and have offended God. They deserve

24. Yoder, *Shalom*, pp. 53-70.

punishment since punishment is normative and there is no way to make restitution. God cannot simply forgive because that would represent the failure of retributive justice. A debt is owed, and Jesus offered himself as a substitute. The context of this approach, then, is clearly retributive rather than shalom justice.

The usual translation and use of Romans 5:1-11 illustrates this perspective. The opening words of this passage are about peace and justice, but training and translation has obscured this dimension.[25] They are usually translated, "Therefore, since we are *justified* by faith, we have peace with God" (RSV). Most Protestants have focused on *justification*, interpreting it as an act by which God proclaims us innocent even though we are not. A judicial proceeding, a legal fiction, is at the heart of atonement, and it required God's action, not ours. Lois Barrett notes that a more faithful translation of the passage might be, "Therefore, since we come into right relationship through faith (or faithfulness). . . ." The Old Testament background from which Paul worked was that of covenant justice. The atonement takes on new dimensions in that light.

Thus a grounding in shalom presents a different view of atonement, one which brings into harmony Christ's life and death and the larger scope of biblical history. Christ's life is an attempt to move humanity toward shalom, toward the kingdom of God. This brought him in conflict with established authorities, resulting in his death. But Christ arose, and the resurrection is a sign: a sign that suffering love is victorious over evil, a sign that good will triumph in the long run. Christ's life provides a model of shalom living.

---

25. See Lois Barrett, "The Gospel of Peace," MCC *Peace Section Newsletter*, 18, No. 2 (March-April, 1988), pp. 1-8.

His death and resurrection are harbingers of future liberation, a sign that shalom is possible.

Drawing upon the sacrificial symbolism of the old covenant, a new covenant is affirmed. Characteristic of covenant justice, God offers forgiveness—not because we have earned it or deserve it—but because God loves us. The slate can in fact be wiped clean.

Whether the thrust of the Bible is on retribution or restoration is not a marginal issue. The question is at the heart of our understandings about the nature of God and about the nature of God's actions in history. It is not an issue which Christians can avoid.

CHAPTER 9

VORP:
An Experimental Plot

On May 28, 1974, two young men from Elmira, Ontario, pleaded guilty to vandalizing 22 properties.[1] No one could have guessed that their cases would lead to a movement with international dimensions.

Several days earlier a group of Christians had met to talk about a Christian response to shoplifting. The Elmira case had been widely publicized and so came up in the discussion. Probation officer Mark Yantzi, whose responsibility it was to prepare the presentence report in the case, was present. "Wouldn't it be neat," he dreamed, "for these offenders to meet the victims?" Knowing it was impossible, Mark dropped the idea.

But Dave Worth, coordinator of Voluntary Service workers for Mennonite Central Committee (MCC) in Kitchener, Ontario, would not let the idea go. Frustrated with the usual process and interested in making peacemaking practical, he announced, "I am ready for a pie-in-the-sky idea." Mark, also a Mennonite, had orig-

---

1. John Bender recounts this story in "Peace Section Newsletter," 16, No. 1 (January-February, 1986), pp. 1-5. So also does Dean Peachey, "The Kitchener Experiment," *Mediation and Criminal Justice: Victims, Offenders and Community*, eds. Martin Wright and Burt Galaway (London: Sage Publications Ltd., 1989), pp. 14-26.

inally been placed in the probation department through a cooperative arrangement with MCC. His mandate was to help explore community-oriented alternatives. He was open to new ideas, but he had doubts. "Do I want to risk my reputation in suggesting a negotiated settlement between the victim and these offenders that has no basis in law?" he wondered. Mark decided to take a chance and so he proposed to the judge that the offenders meet and pay back the victims.

The judge's first response was predictable: "That can't be done." To Mark and Dave's surprise, however, when the time for sentencing arrived, face-to-face meetings between victim and offender to work out restitution were exactly what the judge ordered. Accompanied by their probation officers or the volunteer coordinator, the two boys visited the homes of all but the two victims who had moved. Restitution was negotiated, and within months repayment had been made. From this beginning the victim-offender reconciliation movement was born in Canada. In the U.S. the movement came to birth through a project started in Elkhart, Indiana, in 1977-78.

In the Elmira case, the approach was simplistic. "We were pretty brutal," Mark remembers. "We walked up to the door. They [the boys] knocked. We stood back with our note pads." Fortunately, both the approach and the underlying philosophy of the Victim Offender Reconciliation Program (or "VORP") have been much refined since that time.

Although approaches and names vary, there are today at least 100 programs in the United States using victim-offender mediation, a primary element in VORP.[2] Several dozen programs exist in Canada. Relat-

---

2. Mark Umbreit, "Mediation of Victim Offender Conflict," *Journal of Dispute Resolution*, 1988, pp. 85-105.

ed programs are also operating in England, as well as a number of countries in continental Europe, including Germany, France, Finland, and Holland.[3] Not all of these trace their roots back to VORP itself. About 60 percent of the programs in the U.S., for example, are thought to be explicitly tied to the VORP tradition. Taken together, however, these programs provide a broad base of experience for an approach which combines within a criminal justice framework elements of mediation and reparative justice. A large variety of dispute resolution programs have now sprung up, some of which handle cases with potential or actual criminal justice involvement. These have provided an additional reservoir of experience.

The VORP Concept

In its "classic" form as pioneered in Kitchener, Ontario, and Elkhart, Indiana, VORP is an independent organization outside the criminal justice system. But it works in cooperation this system.[4] This VORP process

---

3. Some of the dimensions of this movement are treated in Wright and Galaway, *Mediation and Criminal Justice*; and in Tony F. Marshall, *Alternatives to Criminal Courts: The Potential for Non-Judicial Dispute Settlement* (Brookfield, Vermont: Gower Publishing Co., 1985). PACT, Inc., 254 S. Morgan Blvd., Valparaiso, IN 46383, periodically publishes a directory of U.S. programs.

4. General descriptions of VORP may be found in Howard Zehr and Earl Sears, *Mediating the Victim-Offender Conflict* (Akron, Pennsylvania: Mennonite Central Committee, 1982); Wright and Galaway, *Mediation and Criminal Justice*; Howard Zehr and Mark Umbreit, "Victim Offender Reconciliation: An Incarceration Substitute?" *Federal Probation*, XXXXVI, No. 4 (December 1982), 63-68; Mark Umbreit, *Crime and Reconciliation: Creative Options for Victims and Offenders* (Nashville: Abingdon Press, 1985). More detailed information is available in *The VORP Book: An Organizational and Operations Manual*, Howard Zehr, ed., available from PACT, Inc. (see previous note).

In the U.S., VORP resources are available from PACT and from the MCC U.S. Office of Criminal Justice, 107 W. Lexington, Elkhart, IN 46516. In Canada they are available from the Network for Community Justice and Conflict Resolution, 298 Frederick St., Kitchener, Ontario N2H 2N5. In England, write to FIRM, 19 London End, Beaconsfield, Bucks HP9 2HN.

consists of a face-to-face encounter between victim and offender in cases which have entered the criminal justice process and the offender has admitted the offense. In these meetings, emphasis is upon three elements: facts, feelings, and agreements. The meeting is facilitated and chaired by a trained mediator, preferably a community volunteer.

Third-party facilitators or mediators play an extremely important role in this process, but they are trained not to impose their own interpretations or solutions. Meetings are conducted in an atmosphere which provides some structure, yet allows participants rather than facilitators to determine outcomes. Both parties are encouraged to tell their stories. Both get a chance to ask questions, to discover from the other just what happened. They also talk about the impact and implications of this experience. When they have done this, they decide together what will be done about it. Once they come to agreement, they sign a written contract. Often this takes the form of financial restitution, but that is not the only possibility.

Offenders may agree to work for victims. Sometimes victims ask rather that offenders work for the community, and may sign a community service agreement. Or they may agree to a certain behavior. If the incident involved people who knew one another previously, such an agreement might specify how they will behave to one another in the future.

These encounters can be important experiences for both victims and offenders. Victims receive a unique opportunity to "get the facts," to ask the questions that bother them. They can also talk about what the offense meant to them *and* to the one who did it. Since they are able to meet the actual person involved, stereotypes are challenged and fears are often reduced. Not only do they receive an opportunity to be repaid for losses, they also have input into what that repayment will be. Thus VORP provides opportunity for expression of feelings, exchange of information, and recovery of losses while leaving victims with a sense of empowerment.

Offenders receive an opportunity to put a real face to those they have harmed. They learn firsthand the consequences of their actions. Stereotypes and rationalizations are confronted directly. In this way—and by being encouraged to take responsibility for making things right—they are held directly accountable for what they have done. They are provided opportunity to bring emotional closure to the offense by actions to make things right and, if they wish to do so, by expressing remorse or seeking forgiveness. Because they are real participants rather than bystanders, they too can experience empowerment.

Victim-offender encounters to discuss the offense and its resolution are the heart of the VORP process, but important work goes on before and after such meetings. Victim and offender are contacted separately first. This provides them with an opportunity to express their feelings and needs and to decide whether they wish to participate. If they choose to do so, a meeting is arranged. After the meeting, there is follow-up to do. A staff person must monitor contracts, making sure they are fulfilled, and do some trouble-shooting if they break down. Some programs are also instituting final victim-offender meetings to bring final closure to the case once agreements have been fulfilled.

Most VORP cases are referred by courts, although

there are exceptions. Some programs receive referrals from the police. Sometimes victims or offenders initiate contact. Cases may be handled as a diversion from prosecution, but in its "classic" form in the U.S., the program takes most referrals from the court, with the agreement becoming the sentence or part of it. For court-referred cases, offenders often go on probation while their contract is being fulfilled.

The majority of cases handled by VORPs in the U.S. and Canada have been property cases, with burglaries being a common offense. Burglary in fact is a good case for the VORP process. While the "system" often treats burglary as a fairly minor offense, victims experience burglary much like a violent personal attack. A meeting with an offender provides an opportunity to vent feelings, to find out what really happened, and to meet the actual person. (Why my house? What if I had been home? What happened to the property that was of such sentimental value?) Fears are often reduced and stereotypes modified. Because there are material losses, discussions about restitution provide a concrete focus for the meeting.

But nonproperty offenses are handled as well. A few programs are beginning to handle cases of violence with some regularity.[5]

A program in Winnipeg, Manitoba, focuses primarily on assault cases, and a few programs work carefully with incidents of serious violence including homicide. A study of British programs has found that the seriousness of the offense is not the determining factor in deciding whether a case can be handled successfully through this process.

---

5. See Mark Umbreit, "Violent Offenders and Their Victims," in *Mediation and Criminal Justice*, eds. Wright and Galaway, pp. 99-112.

What Has Been Learned?

Most research findings so far have been encouraging. While only about one half of all referrals end in meetings (and this figure is consistent with statistics for mediation programs generally), nearly all meetings result in an agreement.[6]

Moreover, unlike nonmediated restitution contracts, most of these agreements are fulfilled—the figure is normally above 80 or even 90 percent.

One study of VORPs in the American Midwest found that only 11 percent of victims who participated expressed some dissatisfaction. Ninety-seven percent reported that they would do it again and would recommend it to friends.[7] All victims in a smaller but more recent study of the Langley, British Columbia, VORP said they would choose to participate again.[8] Substantial victim satisfaction, then, is apparent.

Victims give a variety of reasons for participating, but going into the process many note the importance of restitution. After the VORP experience, however, other benefits loom larger for them. In a study of burglaries in Minneapolis, for example, victims reported that the most important benefit was meeting the offender. Sometimes this allayed fears, reduced stereotypes, or gave them a chance to see to it that the offender got

6. Interestingly, the percentage of referrals which actually come to meetings is in a similar range (40-60%) for most types of mediation programs. One look at reasons why cases do not come to meetings is John Gehm, "Mediated Victim-Offender Restitution Agreements: An Exploratory Analysis of Factors Related to Victim Participation," (Valparaiso, Indiana: PACT Institute of Justice, 1988).

7. Robert B. Coates and John Gehm, *Victim Meets Offender: An Evaluation of Victim-Offender Reconciliation Programs* (Michigan City, Indiana: PACT Institute of Justice, 1985).

8. Andrew Gibson, "Victim-Offender Reconciliation Program: Research Project, Langley, B.C." (Simon Fraser University, 1986).

help. But they also noted the importance of telling what happened and getting answers.[9]

Overall, a sense of participation was the strongest theme in this study. VORP appears to make possible some of the preconditions for healing: empowerment, truth-telling, answering of questions, recovery of losses, even a sense of reassurance. It also provides victims with a chance to feel that they are "doing something" to perhaps help change the offender's behavior, a theme that research has surprisingly found to be important to victims.[10]

Offenders too apparently find satisfaction in participating. All offenders in the Midwestern study cited earlier and 91 percent of offenders in the Langley, B.C., study said that, if they had it to do over, they would go through VORP again. Offenders expressed an increased awareness of victims as people and attitudinal change was measurable in some cases. Nevertheless, they found the experience difficult and talked of it as being tough punishment. Often offenders listed meeting the victim as both the best and the worst part of the process.

Does VORP change offender behavior? Several recent studies have found a reduction in recidivism rates for those who participate. More studies are needed, but Burt Galaway, a leading specialist in restitution, reviewed the literature and concluded that the impact of restitution and VORP on recidivism is as great or great-

9. Mark S. Umbreit and Mike Schumacher, *Victim Understanding of Fairness: Burglary Victims in Victim Offender Mediation* (Minneapolis: Minnesota Citizens Council on Crime and Justice, 1988).

10. For victims' perspectives in England, see Helen Reeves, "The Victim Support Perspective," *Mediation and Criminal Justice,* eds. Wright and Galaway, pp. 44-55 (see esp. pp. 51ff.).

er than that of other sanctions.[11]

VORP practitioners tend to feel that VORP does encourage behavioral changes, but question whether this concern should be central. VORP is important because it addresses the victim-offender relationship and meets some important victim and offender needs that are normally unmet. VORP recognizes the obligations created by crime and even if VORP had no impact on behavior, making things right would be the right thing to do.

But is VORP justice? In the Midwestern study, victims and offenders were asked what justice meant and whether they had experienced it. Almost 80 percent of both victims and offenders who had gone through VORP believed that justice had been served in their cases. Definitions of justice varied, but common themes were "making things right" (a biblical concept!), holding offenders accountable, and "fairness and equity in settling disputes." "To make things right," in fact, was the leading reason given by offenders for participating in the Langley, B.C., program. In the Minneapolis study, the more traditional idea of justice as punishment through imprisonment was the least frequent concern expressed by victims who participated.

The Minneapolis study was small and preliminary, but one of its findings was particularly hopeful. Victims who went through VORP were *twice* as likely to feel that they had been treated fairly by the criminal justice process. Apparently VORP does indeed provide an experience of justice.

In a 1988 article, Burt Galaway surveyed what has been learned from restitution programs, including

---

11. Burt Galaway, "Restitution As Innovation or Unfulfilled Promise?" *Federal Probation*, XII, No. 3 (September 1988), pp. 3-14.

VORP, since the early seventies.[12] His conclusions are encouraging.

Galaway concludes that the experience of the past 16 years indicates unequivocally that such programs can be implemented. Establishing restitution amounts has not been unduly difficult, and repayment rates are high. This includes VORP. Studies show that more than 50 percent of victims are willing to participate. Mediation "is a viable method for arriving at restitution amounts and will be a constructive experience for both victims and offenders."

Restitution and VORP can meet some key goals of the present justice system, Galaway observes. In assuming that people must receive their just deserts, retributive justice looks for a sense of proportionality between offense and penalty. This occurs when participants perceive the outcome to be fair. While research on this is still limited, it appears that restitution is seen as fair and satisfying by victims, offenders, and the general public. It can, therefore, be viewed as just deserts.

Another purpose of punishment is specific deterrence. Do people repeat their offenses? A growing body of evidence suggests that restitution, including VORP, has as an impact on recidivism as great as or greater than other sanctions.

Both victims and the general public will support the use of restitution. A variety of studies show that the public approves of reparative sanctions and that they, as well as victims, support moves toward noncustodial sanctions which include restitution. Moreover, programs such as VORP can provide information to victims about their cases and give them a sense of partici-

---

12. Galaway, "Restitution as Innovation or Unfulfilled Promise?"

pation. Studies show these to be important victim concerns.

Given these findings, Galaway concludes that restitution programs such as VORP should begin to replace other penalties within the current justice system. The Canadian Parliament's Committee on Justice and the Solicitor General have taken steps in that direction.[13] In August 1988, they released a report on sentencing, corrections, and parole entitled "Taking Responsibility." This report describes VORP and its benefits and recommends legislative changes to facilitate and encourage this approach. One recommendation suggests the following unusual purpose of sentence be enacted:

> The purpose of sentencing is to contribute to the maintenance of a just, peaceful, and safe society by holding offenders accountable for their criminal conduct through the imposition of just sanctions which
>
> a. require, or encourage when it is not possible to require, offenders to acknowledge the harm they have done to victims and the community, and to take responsibility for the consequences of their behavior.
>
> b. take account of the steps offenders have taken, or propose to take, to make reparations to the victim and/or the community for the harm done or to otherwise demonstrate acceptance of responsibility.

13. "Taking Responsibility: Report of the Standing Committee on Justice and Solicitor General on Sentencing, Conditional Release, and Related Aspects of Corrections," David Daubney, chairman. Summary and excerpts in "Justice," November 1988, a publication of the Church Council on Justice and Corrections, 507 Bank St., Ottawa, Ontario K2P 1Z5, Canada.

c. facilitate victim-offender reconciliation where victims so request, or are willing to participate in such programs.

d. if necessary, provide offenders with opportunities which are likely to facilitate their habilation or rehabilitation as productive and law-abiding members of society; and

e. if necessary, denounce the behavior and/or incapacitate the offender.

"Taking Responsibility" looks specifically at victim concerns and recognizes that to define crime as an offense against the state "fails to recognize the victim's suffering and feelings of injustice." It goes on to say that "there are five main things necessary to allow victims to restore their sense of worth and get on with their lives." These are described as information, support, recognition of the harm, reparation for the harm, and effective protection.

As the following excerpt shows, the Committee acknowledged the concept of restorative justice.

The proponents of the concept of restorative justice have long recognized the importance to both the victim and the offender (and thereby, ultimately, to the community) of offenders accepting responsibility for their actions and taking steps to repair the harm done.

Goals Are Important

A VORP approach clearly has the potential to address a number of needs. However, the movement as a whole has been challenged to be clear about its values and goals. Is the primary goal to be an alternative? To reform offenders? To help victims? To involve the community? To punish offenders? The goals which VORP chooses to pursue make a great deal of difference in how it operates in practice.

In fact, the movement has been reminded its goals are sometimes unclear and that some of these goals may be mutually contradictory. Programs need to choose one overriding goal and to be clear about the implications of this decision for its other goals and its operations.

If a primary purpose is to reform offenders or to mitigate their punishment, VORPs may easily come to neglect victims' needs and perspectives, even if VORP claims to take victims seriously. This criticism has emerged from evaluations of some British programs.[14] If VORPs seek primarily to provide an alternative to prison, they will concentrate primarily upon serious, prison-bound cases—to the neglect of more "minor" cases which may have serious implications for victim and offender or their relationships. Clarity about and priorities among goals are important.

Some VORPs have ignored this question and others have answered in various ways. The Elkhart program concluded that its one main goal was reconciliation. The staff recognized this to be a strange-sounding goal in the world of criminal justice and that reconciliation is hard to define. Nevertheless, reconciliation as a goal signifies that the victim-offender relationship is the primary focus of the process. Once that was decided, program operations had to be redesigned to reflect this focus. Volunteers had to be trained, for example, not just

14. The British Home Office has sponsored extensive quantitative and qualitative research on the VORP or "reparations" projects there. I am indebted to Tony Marshall—who oversaw this research for the Home Office—for summaries of the results. Publication is planned.

to secure an agreement, but to encourage the expression of feelings and attitudes.

A decision to make reconciliation (or at least *opportunities* for reconciliation) does not mean that other potential benefits do not exist or should not be pursued, but that they are secondary. VORP practitioners believe, for example, that the personal accountability which VORP offers can change offender's attitudes and behavior. Yet this is not the primary goal. The process is worth doing even if attitudes and behaviors are not changed. An offense harms a person, and creates an obligation to that person. A just response, then, involves some attempt to make it right. It is the "right" thing to do, regardless of its other impacts.

VORP's focus on an unconventional goal such as reconciliation is the source of some tension with the criminal justice system. How do we mesh a process which is reparative in focus with one that is retributive? Can it be done, or will the larger system in the end overwhelm the smaller? Can VORP help transform the retributively oriented criminal justice system, or will the system transform VORP? Will VORP go the way of so many other "alternatives," perhaps even become a new instrument of control and punishment?

These are genuine questions and researchers are sounding some warnings in this area. Some programs, for example, have come to reflect the system's offender orientation and have neglected victims. Reconciliation is sometimes replaced as a goal by more familiar goals such as accountability or even restitution. Many are beginning to downplay reconciliation as a goal and are emphasizing mediation, the process.

A recent study of English programs warns of the dangers of tacking new experiments onto the existing criminal justice system.[15] This includes even (or espe-

15. Gwynn Davis, Jacky Boucherat, and David Watson, *A Preliminary Study*

cially!) reparative ones. At minimum, they remind us that we must keep value questions in the forefront. They call for a new understanding and language of justice and for research which will shape and test the viability of a reparative paradigm.

VORP as a Catalyst

Since 1978, I have been a participant in the VORP movement. Initially, my participation was resistant and skeptical. Through previous work in criminal justice I had developed a perspective which I considered quite critical. And I suspected that VORP did not sufficiently challenge basic premises. As I experienced VORP firsthand, however, I came to realize that the parameters of my earlier "critical" framework were in fact quite conventional. It was VORP which had the potential to transform my ideas about justice.

In my earlier work with prisoners and defendants, I had not understood the perspectives of victims. Indeed, I did not want to, for they served primarily as interference in the process of finding "justice" for the offender. I did not fundamentally question the state's role in justice, nor did I ask whether the administration of pain was the proper focus. I was, however, well aware of the many and often systematic injustices in the way criminal justice selects and treats offenders.

VORP forced me to meet and listen to crime victims, and that caused me to begin rethinking what crime is and what ought to happen. The experience of seeing two hostile people—victim and offender—leave a meeting with new understandings of what happened could

of Victim Offender Mediation and Reparation Schemes in England and Wales, Research and Planning Unit Paper 42 (London: Home Office, 1987), pp. 60-65.

not help but leave an impact. Often they left with new understandings of each other, sometimes with new, even friendly, relationships. Eventually the implications of all this began to sink in. VORP has become, for me, the agent of a transformation of my understanding of justice and a demonstration that such justice is not just theoretical but can be practical. Yet the implementation and spread of VORP has also posed important questions and raised some warning flags.

When agriculturists want to solve certain problems in crops, they often experiment with new strains. To do that, they test by planting them in experimental plots. When such plots are successful, they may become demonstration plots to help persuade others to try. Since 1974, VORP has served as both an experimental and a demonstration plot.[16] VORP's demonstration role is important: VORP serves as a reminder that there are other ways to understand and respond to crime—that justice can repair. But the experimental role must not be abandoned. VORP itself must continue to experiment, to push out new boundaries. We need new experiments that go beyond VORP—experiments which will help develop and test new understandings of crime and justice.

In planting and nursing such plots, the church's role is critical. Although the VORP movement is well established in the world at large by now, the church played a pivotal role in its development and spread, and still remains deeply involved in many communities. That is as it should be. VORP embodies a vision of justice that is inherently biblical and thus provides an arena where the church can implement its vision.

---

16. Credit for the "plot" analogy goes to Clarence Jordan and John H. Yoder.

The VORP movement desperately needs the church if it is to survive in a form that matters. Pressures to be sidetracked from the vision are many. The church can provide the kind of independent value base and independent institutional base which is necessary to carry the vision. Motivated by a biblical vision of justice as restoration, perhaps the church can continue to plant plots which will experiment and demonstrate another way. If VORP is to survive as a catalyst for change, the church must remain involved.

PART IV

A New Lens

CHAPTER 10

A Restorative Lens

As I am thinking about writing this chapter, I take time out to go to court. An eighteen-year-old boy, my neighbor, is scheduled to be sentenced. He has pleaded guilty to molesting the young girl next door. Her mother has asked for my help. She doesn't want him to go to prison where he might become a victim himself, but she wants the behavior to stop. "If it were anyone else," she tells me, "I would want to string him up. But Ted just needs help."

Ted has bothered children before, including one of my daughters.

"I'm going to continue this sentencing until a later date," says the judge. "Frankly, I don't know what to do. Howard, maybe you can help."

Where does one start in this sort of case? I begin by framing the issues in a conventional way. He's broken the law. What does the law require? What will the court accept? What should the court do with him? Then I remember what I've been writing, and my framework begins to shift.

The framework: it makes a difference. How do we interpret what has happened? What factors are relevant? What responses are possible and appropriate?

The lens we look through determines how we frame both the problem and the "solution." That lens is the focus of this book.

I have been involved in photography for many years. One of the lessons I have learned is how profoundly the lens I look through affects the outcome. My choice of lens determines in what circumstances I can work and how I see. If I choose a "slow" lens with a small maximum aperture, the image will be dim and good-quality photographs may be hard to obtain under low light levels.

The focal length of the lens also makes a difference. A wide-angle lens is highly inclusive. It incorporates within the frame a multitude of subjects, but it does so at the cost of a certain distortion. Objects which are nearer become large, leaving objects in the background small. Also, the shapes of objects at the corners of the frame are altered. Circles become ellipses.

A telephoto lens is more selective. The scope of its vision is narrower, incorporating fewer objects within the frame. It too "distorts," but in a different way than a wide-angle lens. With a telephoto lens, objects are larger but distances are compressed. Objects appear closer to the camera—and closer to one another—than they are to the naked eye.

The choice of lens, then, affects what is in the picture. It also determines the relationships and proportions of the elements included. Similarly, the lens we use to examine crime and justice affects what we include as relevant variables, what we consider their relative importance to be, and what we consider proper outcomes.

We view crime through a retributive lens. The "criminal justice" process which uses that lens fails to meet many of the needs of either victim or offender. The process neglects victims while failing to meet its expressed goals of holding offenders accountable and deterring crime.

Such failures have led to the widespread sense of crisis today. An array of reforms have been attempted. The fads of today such as electronic monitoring and intensive supervision are simply the most recent of a long line of "solutions." Yet this system has shown itself remarkably resistant to significant improvement, absorbing and subverting efforts at reform. A French proverb seems true: "The more things change, the more they remain the same."

The reason for such failure, I am arguing, lies in our choice of lens: that is, in the assumptions we make about crime and justice. These assumptions, which govern our responses to wrongdoing, are in fact out of step with the experience of crime. Furthermore, they are out of step with our Christian roots and even with much of our own history in the West. To find our way out of this maze, we will have to look beyond alternative punishments, and even beyond alternatives to punishment. We will have to look to alternative ways of viewing both problem and solution. Professor Kay Harris, a specialist in sentencing, has reminded us that it is a matter of alternate values, not of alternate technologies of punishment.[1]

Our failures are negative signposts which identify a need for change, but there are positive signposts which point a direction. The experiences and needs of victims and offenders indicate some of the concerns we must address. The biblical tradition offers some principles.

---

1. See M. Kay Harris, "Strategies, Values and the Emerging Generation of Alternatives to Incarceration," *New York University Review of Law and Social Change*, XII, No. 1 (1983-4), 141-170, and "Observations of a 'Friend of the Court' on the Future of Probation and Parole," *Federal Probation*, LI, No. 4 (December 1987), pp. 12-21.

Our historical experience and more recent "experimental plots" suggest possible approaches. Perhaps these signposts can serve as elements for a new lens.

A new lens, perhaps, but a new paradigm as well? A paradigm is more than a vision or a proposal. It requires well-articulated theory, combined with a consistent grammar and a "physics" of application—and some degree of consensus. It need not solve all problems, but it must solve the most pressing ones and must point a direction. I doubt that we are there yet.

More realistic at this stage are alternative visions, rooted in both principle and experience, which can help to guide our search for solutions to the present crisis. We can adopt a different lens, even though it cannot as yet be a full-fledged paradigm. Such visions can help give direction to what must be a shared journey of experimentation and exploration.

In this search, we are seeking a vision of what the standard ought to be, what is normative, not what would be a realistic response in all situations. The current lens builds upon the unusual, the bizarre. It makes procedures for such cases normative for "ordinary" offenses. Some offenders are so inherently dangerous that they need to be restrained. Someone must make that decision, guided by rules and careful safeguards. Some offenses are so heinous that they require special handling. But these special cases should not set the norm. Our approach, then, should be to identify what crime means and what normally ought to happen when it does, while recognizing the need for certain exceptions. For now, then, we will not preoccupy ourselves with whether our vision can encompass all situations. Rather we will try to envision what ought to be the norm.

One way to start this exploration is to take crime down from its high plane of abstraction. This means understanding it as the Bible understands it and as we experience it: as injury and as a violation of people and of relationships. Justice ought, then, to focus on repairing, on making things right.

In that case, the two contrasting lenses might be sketched like this:

Retributive Justice
Crime is a violation of the state, defined by lawbreaking and guilt. Justice determines blame and administers pain in a contest between the offender and the state directed by systematic rules.

Restorative Justice
Crime is a violation of people and relationships. It creates obligations to make things right. Justice involves the victim, the offender, and the community in a search for solutions which promote repair, reconciliation, and reassurance.

Crime: Violation of People and Relationships

In the first chapter, I pointed out that a person often experiences even minor property crimes as an attack on the self. Victims feel personally violated, even when the direct harm is only to property. The shalom vision reminds us that this material level is important to a sense of well-being.

But the shalom vision also reminds us that crime represents a violation of human relationships. Crime affects our sense of trust, resulting in feelings of suspicion, of estrangement, sometimes of racism. Frequently it creates walls between friends, loved ones, relatives, and neighbors. Crime affects our relationships with those around us.

Crime also represents a ruptured relationship between the victim and offender. Even if they had no previous relationship, the crime creates a relationship.

And that relationship is usually hostile. Left unre-
solved, that hostile relationship in turn affects the well-
being of victim and offender.

Crime represents an injury to the victim but it may
also involve injury to the offender. Much crime grows
out of injury. Many offenders have experienced abuse
as children. Many lack the skills and training that make
meaningful jobs and lives possible. Many seek ways to
feel validated and empowered. For many, crime is a
way of crying for help and asserting their personhood.
They do harm in part because of harm done to them.
Often they are then further harmed in the "justice"
process. This dimension grows in part out of larger distributive justice issues. It also is an integral part of the
shalom vision.

Crime then is at its core a violation of a person by
another person, a person who himself or herself may
be wounded. It is a violation of the just relationship
that should exist between individuals. There is also a
larger social dimension to crime. Indeed, the effects of
crime ripple out, touching many others. Society too has
a stake in the outcome and a role to play. Still, these
public dimensions should not be the starting point.
Crime is not first an offense against society, much less
against the state. Crime is first an offense against people, and it is here that we should start.

This interpersonal dimension of crime reminds us
that crime involves conflict.[2] Indeed, several European
scholars working toward a new lens for viewing crime
have urged us to define crime as a form of conflict.
After all, crime creates interpersonal conflict and some-

---

2. See, e.g., Louk Hulsman's work, cited above. See also John R. Blad,
Hans van Mastrigt, and Niels A. Uldriks, eds., *The Criminal Justice System as
a Social Problem: An Abolitionist Perpective* (Rotterdam, Netherlands: Erasmus
Universiteit, 1987).

times it grows out of conflict. Certainly crime is related to other harms and conflicts in society. Properly approached, many such conflictual situations can be opportunities for learning and growth whether or not one defines them as crimes.

Marie Marshall Fortune has warned that to label crime *conflict* can be misleading and dangerous.[3] In situations of domestic violence, for example, we have too often defined violent acts with serious consequences as simply an outgrowth of conflict. This has tended to mute responsibility for behavior by blaming the victim. It also assumes that violence is simply an escalation of conflict. Violence is not, Fortune reminds us, simply an escalation of conflict. It is categorically different. It is one thing to have a difference of opinion and to argue. It is quite another to attack another physically.

Because of its interpersonal dimensions, crime obviously involves conflict. To equate it with conflict, however, may be misleading and may obscure some important dimensions.

What about the term *crime*? Some would have us avoid the term altogether. *Crime* is a result of a legal system which makes arbitrary distinctions between various harms and conflicts. It is an artificial construct which throws into one basket a variety of unrelated behaviors and experiences. It separates them from other harms and violations and thereby obscures the real meaning of the experience.

Because of this, Dutch criminologist and lawyer Louk Hulsman has suggested the term *problematic situations.*[4]

---

3. Marshall Fortune raised this concern in a consultation on restorative justice and "tough cases" held in Guelph, Ontario, in 1986.

4. Cf. "Critical Criminology and the Concept of Crime," *Contemporary Crises: Law, Crime and Social Policy*, 10 (1986), pp. 63-80.

That term helpfully reminds us of the connection between "crimes" and other types of harms and conflicts. It also suggests the learning possibilities that are inherent in such situations. But *problematic situations* feels vague and, for serious harms, may seem to minimize the dimensions of the hurt. Certainly it is difficult to imagine "problematic situations" taking the place of "crime" in ordinary discussion!

An alternate term would be helpful, but so far I have not found an acceptable replacement. So for now I'll stick to *crime*, keeping in mind its inadequacies.

Crime involves injuries which need healing. Those injuries represent four basic dimensions of harm:

1. To the victim
2. To interpersonal relationships
3. To the offender
4. To the community

The retributive lens focuses primarily on the latter, social dimensions. It does so in a way that makes *community* abstract and impersonal. Retributive justice defines the state as victim, defines wrongful behavior as violation of rules, and sees the relationship between victim and offender as irrelevant. *Crimes*, then, are categorically different from other types of wrongs.

A restorative lens identifies people as victims and recognizes the centrality of the interpersonal dimensions. Offenses are defined as personal harms and interpersonal relationships. Crime is a violation of people and of relationships.

Understandings of Crime

Retributive Lens	*Restorative Lens*
Crime defined by violation of rules (i.e., broken rules)	Crime defined by harm to people and relationships (i.e., broken relationships)

Harms defined abstractly	Harms defined concretely
Crime seen as categorically different from other harms	Crime recognized as related to other harms and conflicts
State as victim	People and relationships as victims
State and offender seen as primary parties	Victim and offender seen as primary parties
Victims' needs and rights ignored	Victims' needs and rights central
Interpersonal dimensions irrelevant	Interpersonal dimensions central
Conflictual nature of crime obscured	Conflictual nature of crime recognized
Wounds of offender peripheral	Wounds of offender important
Offense defined in technical, legal terms	Offense understood in full context: moral, social, economic, political

So far we've limited most of our discussion to the harms and conflicts that we usually label as crimes. Such a narrow focus, however, is not biblical. The Bible holds out for us a vision of how people ought to live together, in a state of shalom, of right relationship. Behaviors we call crime violate such relationships, but so do a variety of other harms, including acts of injustice and oppression by the powerful against the powerless. To be biblical in our understanding, we will have to see injustice holistically, without artificial lines between crimes and other injustices. We must see the whole continuum of harms. Crimes merge into other harms and conflicts between individuals that we normally term *civil*. But those injustices join with injustices of power and wealth. The Old Testament prophets remind us that structural injustice is sin, and that such injustice in turn breeds more injustice.

Restoration: The Goal

If crime is injury, what is justice? Again, a biblical understanding points the way. If crime harms people, justice should be a search to make things right to and between people. When a wrong occurs, the central question ought not to be, "What should be done to the offender?" or "What does the offender deserve?" Instead, the primary question ought to be, "What can be done to make things right?"

Instead of defining justice as retribution, we will define justice as restoration. If crime is injury, justice will repair injuries and promote healing. Acts of restoration —not further harm—will counterbalance the harm of crime. We cannot guarantee full recovery, of course, but true justice would aim to provide a context in which the process can begin.

If the harm of crime has four dimensions, reparative energies ought to address these dimensions. The first goal of justice, then, ought to be restitution and healing for victims.

Healing for victims does not imply that one can or should forget or minimize the violation. Rather, it implies a sense of recovery, a degree of closure. The violated should again begin to feel like life makes some sense and that they are safe and in control. The violator should be encouraged to change. He or she should receive freedom to begin life anew. Healing encompasses a sense of recovery and a hope for the future.

Healing of the relationship between victim and offender should be a second major concern of justice. The victim-offender reconciliation movement has identified this goal as reconciliation.

Reconciliation implies full repentance and forgiveness. It involves establishing a positive relationship between the victim and offender. The VORP experience suggests that this is possible. Yet it would be unrealistic to expect reconciliation to occur in all cases. In many cases, nothing like reconciliation will be accomplished. In other cases, a satisfactory relationship may be worked out that does not imply intimacy or complete trust. In no way should participants feel coerced toward reconciliation. Ron Kraybill, former director of Mennonite Conciliation Service, has reminded us that reconciliation has a rhythm and dynamic of its own. Even if we consciously want reconciliation, our emotions may go a different direction.

> To the brain's concern with what *ought* to be, the heart responds with what *is*. The head *can* set a direction for the heart, but the heart must arrive at its own pace. Heart reconciliation is a cycle with stages along the way.[5]

According to Ron Claassen, director of the VORP in Fresno, California, we must see reconciliation as a continuum.[6] On the one end is outright hostility. On the other is the restoration or creation of a strong, positive relationship. When a crime occurs, the relationship is

---

5. Ron Kraybill, "From Head to Heart: The Cycle of Reconciliation," Mennonite Conciliation Service *Conciliation Quarterly*, 7, No. 4 (Fall, 1988), p. 2.

6. Ron Claassen and Howard Zehr, *VORP Organizing: A Foundation in the Church* (Elkhart, Indiana: Mennonite Central Committee, 1988), p. 5.

usually at the hostile end of the scale. Left unaddressed, the relationship usually remains there or even moves toward deeper hostility. The aim of justice, then, ought to be to move the relationship toward reconciliation. Such healing of relationships, even if only partial, is an important step toward healing for individuals. Justice cannot guarantee or force reconciliation, but it ought to provide opportunities for such reconciliation to occur.

I have been involved in VORP cases where little progress toward a reconciled relationship seems to have occurred. Having met to discuss the offense and its resolution, victim and offender remained hostile. Yet the nature of their hostility had changed. No longer were they mad at an abstraction, at a stereotype of a victim or offender. They were now mad at a concrete person. Even that represents some improvement.

Offenders too need healing. They must be accountable for their behavior, of course. They cannot be "let off the hook." Yet this accountability can itself be a step toward change and healing. And their other needs must receive attention.

The community also needs healing. Crime undermines a community's sense of wholeness, and that injury needs to be addressed.

The experience of justice is a basic human need. Without such an experience, healing and reconciliation are difficult or even impossible. Justice is a precondition for closure.

A full sense of justice may, of course, be rare. However, even "approximate justice" can help.[7] Even a par-

---

7. Marie Marshall Fortune suggested this terminology at the Guelph consultation. Cf. Fortune, "Making Justice: Sources of Healing for Incest Survivors," *Working Together*, Summer, 1987, p. 5; and "Justice-Making in the Aftermath of Woman-Battering," *Domestic Violence on Trial*, ed. Daniel Sonkin (New York: Springer Publishers, 1987), pp. 237-248.

tial experience can lay the groundwork which is necessary for a sense of recovery and closure. For example, when an offender has not been identified, or refuses to take responsibility, the community can play a role in providing an experience of justice. They can truly hear and value victims, agreeing that what happened was wrong and listening and attending to their needs. Approximate justice is better than no justice and aids the process of healing.

How should we envision justice? The blindfolded goddess with balance in hand symbolizes well the impersonal, process-oriented, nature of the contemporary paradigm. What is our alternative?

One possibility is to image justice as healing a wound. My colleague Dave Worth, responding to a draft of this chapter, spelled out this image well:

> New tissue must grow to fill the space where the old was torn away. The proper conditions and nutrients must be present to allow the new to grow. There must be safety and cleanliness and time. Sometimes there is a scar, and sometimes there is impairment. But when it is healed we can move and function and grow. And through our experience of wounding and healing, we can have some understanding of the conditions which brought about that wound and the conditions which brought about that healing. [Then] we can work to change the former and to offer the latter to others who are wounded.

Wilma Derksen, whose daughter was brutally murdered, has suggested still another metaphor which I find even more hopeful. Crime creates an emptiness, so justice is filling a hole.[8]

---

8. Wilma Derksen, "Have You Seen Candace?" (working title), manuscript in preparation for publication.

The biblical approach to justice shows that restorative justice must often be transformative justice.[9] To make things right, it may be necessary not merely to return to situations and people to their original condition, but to go beyond. In cases of wife abuse, for example, it is not enough to make amends for the damages. True justice cannot occur unless people and relationships are transformed into something that is healthy so the injury does not recur. Justice may mean moving in a new direction rather than returning to the situation of the past.

Justice may involve more than filling a hole and leveling it off. The hole may be needed to be heaped up until it overflows. Again Dave Worth summarized this image of justice better than I can.

> Second Corinthians 5:18ff. makes a link between reconciliation and new creation. That is perhaps the essence of reconciliation: something new has happened between two people. Not something based on the way it was in the past, but on the way it should be. Reconciliation is really a forward-looking approach to the problem.

> [Overflowing] is what justice is about. It is not the level-over-the-top kind of legalistic approach to justice that we are talking about. We are not talking about the scales of justice. We are talking about a situation where true justice has occurred which has made a new thing come to pass. A thing which leaves people not lower, not just equal, but full and overflowing so they can go out and spread justice to others around them. Perhaps the problem with the present legalistic approach to justice is that it doesn't heap people up so they have no justice left to give others.

---

9. I am indebted to Marie Marshall Fortune for this term.

Justice Begins with Needs

Justice which aims to fill and overflow must begin by identifying and seeking to meet human needs. With crime, the starting point must be the needs of those violated. When a crime occurs (regardless of whether an "offender" is identified) the first questions ought to be, "Who has been harmed?" "How have they been harmed?" "What are their needs?" Such an approach would, of course, be far from that of retributive justice which first asks, "Who did it?" "What should be done to them?"—and then rarely moves beyond that point.

Victims have a variety of needs which must be met if one is to experience even approximate justice. In many cases, the first and most pressing needs are for support and a sense of safety.

Soon after that, however, come a variety of other needs, some of which I noted in the first chapter. Victims need someone to listen to them. They must have opportunities to tell their story and to vent their feelings, perhaps over and over. They must tell their truth. And they need others to suffer with them, to lament with them the evil that has been done.

Somewhere in the process, victims need to feel vindicated. They need to know that what happened to them was wrong and undeserved and that others recognize this as wrong. They need to know that something has been done to correct the wrong and to reduce the chances of its recurrence. They want to hear others acknowledge their pain and validate their experience.

The language of truth-telling, lament, and vindication may sometimes be harsh and angry. We must accept that and truly hear it. Only then can people move beyond. Mort MacCallum-Paterson has concluded that crime victims' cries of anguish are much like the cries of anguish found so frequently in the Old Testament. Cries of pain and demands for vengeance are "prayer-cries," intended for God's ears, asking for God's sympathy and lament. Often they sound angry and vengeful, but they are not necessarily demands for community action. As one murder victim's father said to Paterson, "We may sound as if we're asking for the death penalty. We really aren't ... but what else can we say?" Paterson observes,

> What else can we say? That's the point. There are no words more ultimate than a blood-cry as a way of expressing the grief, the pain and the rage of the survivors of murder victims. Whether or not those words become active strategizing toward the goal of executing the murderer requires another move. It requires a further decision. Lament as such does not contain the decision, but ... lament does contain the *language*. It takes the form of a curse. In effect, it is a prayer that God will damn that one who took the life of the victim.[10]

Retribution may be one form of vindication, but so also is restitution. In an important little book entitled *Mending Hurts*, John Lampen of Northern Ireland notes that restitution is at least as basic a human response as is retribution.[11]

Restitution represents recovery of losses, but its real importance is symbolic. Restitution implies an acknowledgment of the wrong and a statement of responsibility. Making right is itself a form of vindication, a form which may promote healing better than retribution.

Retribution often leaves a legacy of hatred. Perhaps it is more satisfying as an experience of justice than no

---

10. Morton MacCallum-Paterson, "Blood Cries: Lament, Wrath and the Mercy of God," *Touchstone*, May 1987, p. 19.

11. John Lampen, *Mending Hurts* (London: Quaker Home Service, 1987), p. 57.

justice at all, but it does little to address hostilities. Such hostilities can impede healing. That is the beauty of forgiveness. By addressing hostilities, it allows both the victim and the offender to take control of their own lives. Like reconciliation, however, forgiveness is not easy and cannot be forced. For many an experience of justice is a necessary precondition for forgiveness to occur. For some, forgiveness will not seem possible.

Both retribution and restitution have to do with righting an imbalance. While both retribution and restoration have symbolic importance, however, restitution is a more concrete way to restore equity. Also, retribution seeks to right the balance by lowering the offender to the level to which the victim has been reduced. It tries to defeat the wrongdoer, annulling his or her claim to superiority and confirming the victim's sense of worth. Restitution, on the other hand, seeks to raise the victim to his or her previous level. It recognizes his or her moral worth and acknowledges the role of the offender and possibilities for repentance. It thereby acknowledges the moral worth of the offender as well.[12]

Most of us assume that retribution is high on victims' agenda. Recent surveys of victims, however, suggest a different picture. Victims are often open to non-incarcerative, reparative sentences—more frequently, in fact, than is the public.[13]

Moreover, they often rank rehabilitation for the offender as an important value. Help for the offender, after all, is one way of addressing the problem of safety and the prevention of future wrongs.

---

12. Cf. Jeffrie G. Murphy and Jean Hampton, *Forgiveness and Mercy* (Cambridge, England: Cambridge University Press, 1988).

13. See, for example, Russ Immarigeon, "Surveys Reveal Broad Support for Alternative Sentencing," *National Prison Project Journal*, No. 9 (Fall, 1986), pp. 1-4.

Victims also need to be empowered. Justice cannot simply be done to and for them. They must feel needed and listened to in the process. Since one dimension of the wrong was that they were robbed of power, one dimension of justice is to return power to them. At minimum, this means they must be a key in determining what their needs are, how they should be met, and when they should be addressed. But victims should have some role in the overall process.

Victims need reassurance, reparation, vindication, empowerment, but they especially need to find meaning. Remember Ignatieff's insight: justice provides a framework for meaning. Victims need to find answers to questions about what happened, why, and what is being done about it. They need to address the six questions which I suggested in chapter 1 that provide steps to recovery. Only the victims themselves can answer some of these questions, although it may be that we can help them in their search. However, some of these questions are questions of fact. Who did it, why, what kind of person are they, what is being done about it? At minimum, justice should provide such information.

Thus victims often seek vindication. This vindication includes denunciation of the wrong, lament, truth-telling, deprivitization, and deminimization. They seek equity, including reparation, reconciliation, and forgiveness. They sense a need for empowerment, including participation and safety. Another need is reassurance, including support, "suffering with," safety, clarification of responsibility, and prevention. And they have a need for meaning, including information, fairness, answers, and a sense of proportion.

Victims feel violated by crime, and these violations generate needs. Communities feel violated as well, however, and they have needs too. Since one cannot ignore the public dimensions of crime, the justice process in many cases cannot be fully private. The community, too, wants reassurance that what happened was wrong, that something is being done about it, and that steps are being taken to discourage its recurrence. Here too information can be important as it can help to reduce stereotypes and unfounded fears. Here too restitution can play an important role by providing a symbol of the restoration of wholeness. In fact, the role of symbolism is important. Crime undermines the sense of wholeness in a community. For a community, reparation often requires some sort of symbolic action that contains elements of denunciation of the offense, vindication, reassurance, and repair.

The public dimensions of crime are important, therefore, but they should not be the starting point. Also, the community needs to be challenged in some of its assumptions about crime. One of these assumptions is that full order and safety is possible, at least within the framework of a free society.

At a recent fund-raising party for the organization which operates our local VORP, I sat across a picnic table from a well-to-do young man. A spectacular storm was approaching, and everyone else had abandoned us for the safety of the house. As we sat watching the storm, he asked about the organization to which he had just contributed, and that led to a discussion of justice. He told me with considerable candor of his own internal struggle with the question. He had known since childhood a man who was a perpetual thief. Part of him was concerned about that friend's rehabilitation and well-being. On the other hand, he saw himself as conservative and felt that the thief deserved harsh punishment. "Sometimes," he said, "I think we should do what Iran does—cut off an arm, punish severely. Then we'd be safe." "Perhaps," I replied, "but would you want to live here then?"

Order and freedom are two opposites on a continuum. Complete freedom, at least in the sense of freedom to do whatever we wish without formal or informal controls, would likely be chaotic and unsafe, a Hobbesian world. Complete order, on the other hand, even if it were obtainable, would come at the price of freedom. If harsh punishment were to deter crime, for instance, it would have to be swift and sure. The price? We would have to be willing to make mistakes and to give arbitrary power to central authorities—a power which would surely be misused. Most of us would not wish to live in such a world. So we find ourselves moving back and forth somewhere in the middle of that continuum, seeking to balance freedom and order. The conservatives among us find themselves closer to the order end, the liberals closer to the freedom end.

There is yet another error in usual assumptions about freedom and order. Most of the time we think of order as rules and penalties, formal controls. We forget, however, that throughout history order has been maintained by informal controls—by belief systems, by social pressures and obligations, by the rewards of conforming. This is true also in our own everyday lives. To assume that order derives simply from laws and punishment is to overlook what holds society together.

The point in all this is that we cannot live in complete safety and retain other values which we hold dear. At the same time, our freedom is also at risk when we do not call people to account when their attempt to exercise their will infringes on the freedom of others.

Crime Creates Obligations

A discussion of needs quickly leads to questions of

responsibility and liability. Violations create obligations.

The primary obligation, of course, is on the part of the one who has caused the violation. When someone wrongs another, he or she has an obligation to make things right. This is what justice should be about. It means encouraging offenders to understand and acknowledge the harm they have done and then taking steps, even if incomplete or symbolic, to make that wrong right.

Making right is central to justice. Making right is not a marginal, optional activity. It is an obligation. Ideally, the justice process can help offenders to acknowledge and assume their responsibilities willingly. This can happen. It often does in the VORP process. More often, however, persons accept this responsibility reluctantly at first. Many offenders are reluctant to make themselves vulnerable by trying to understand the consequences of their action. After all, they have built up edifices of stereotypes and rationalizations to protect themselves against exactly this kind of information. Many are reluctant to take on the responsibility to make right. In many ways taking one's punishment is easier. While it may hurt for a time, it involves no responsibility and no threat to rationalizations and stereotypes. Offenders often need strong encouragement or even coercion to accept their obligations.

The VORP movement in North America and in England has discussed this often. Obviously this acceptance of responsibility is better when voluntary. Obviously too, coercion can be abused. Still, in principle I do not object to the requirement that offenders must assume their responsibilities. After all, if someone harms someone else, he or she has created a debt, an obligation. The offender should recognize that and willingly accept responsibilities. The justice process should encourage that.

However, persons often will not willingly assume their responsibilities. One of the reasons many offenders get into trouble is a lack of certain kinds of responsibility. One cannot overcome such irresponsibility quickly. What society *can* say to offenders, then, is simple: "You have done wrong by violating someone. You have an obligation to make that wrong right. You may choose to do so willingly, and we will allow you to be involved in figuring out how that should be done. If you do not choose to accept this responsibility, however, we will have to decide for you what needs to be done and will require you to do it."

One can require offenders to accept the obligation to make right. One can strongly encourage them to take fuller responsibility by facing their victims. However, one cannot and must not force them to do so. And one certainly should not coerce victims to participate! Forced encounters are unlikely to be good for either offender or victim, and may well backfire. We can require offenders to make right, but they cannot be fully responsible without some degree of voluntarism.

One purpose of both punishment and reparation is to send messages. The utilitarian aim of punishment is to say to offenders, "Do not commit offenses because they are against the law." "Those who do wrong deserve to get hurt." Reparation or restitution seeks to send a different message. "Don't commit offenses because it harms someone. Those who harm others will have to make it right." The message of our actions does not always sink in, as British author Martin Wright has noted. But when it does, we need to make sure it is the right message.[14]

---

14. "Mediation," (FIRM) 5, No. 2 (March 1989), p. 7.

Regarding the need to send a message that crime is wrong, Wright also observes:

> We can denounce crime more constructively by doing things *for* the victim (and requiring the offenders to do so), rather than *against* the offender.[15]

Crime creates a debt to make right, and that debt remains regardless of whether forgiveness happens. When we offend, we cannot assume that because we have experienced forgiveness from God or even from the one wronged no other obligation remains. Nevertheless, it is also true that victims may choose to forgive even the concrete obligation that is owed. Rarely is an offender able to make up completely for what both the victim and the offender has lost. Herman Bianchi has noted that crime creates a liability, and that forgiveness is about removing the liability for that which cannot be restored.

Insofar as it is possible, offenders should make amends. However, in many cases there are considerable delays before offenders are identified. Often offenders are never identified at all. Also, many of the needs which the victim and the community have as a result of crime are beyond the means of offenders to set right. And offenders have needs as well. This is society's responsibility: to attend to the needs to which individuals alone cannot attend. Certain obligations on the part of the community are thus also generated by crime.

---

15. Martin Wright, "From Retribution to Restoration: A New Model for Criminal Justice," *New Life: The Prison Service Chaplaincy Review*, 5 (1988), p. 49.

Offenders Have Needs Too

Biblically, justice is done not because it is deserved but because it is needed. Although in a retributive or just deserts model offenders may not "deserve" to have their own needs given priority, society's self-interest dictates that these needs be part of a just response. Identifying and addressing offenders' needs is a key element of restorative justice.

In the story with which I opened this chapter, Ted needs to receive treatment. The legal system interprets his behavior as "sexual molestation." This behavior is part of a larger pattern of inadequacy and dysfunction. Left unattended, it will only get worse. Part of the treatment needed involves helping Ted recognize the impact of his actions on his young victim.

Offenders have many needs, of course. They need to have their stereotypes and rationalizations—their "mis-attributions"—about the victim and the event challenged. They may need to learn to be more responsible. They may need to develop employment and interpersonal skills. They often need emotional support. They may need to learn to channel anger and frustration in more appropriate ways. They may need help to develop a positive and healthy self-image. And they often need help in dealing with guilt. Like victims, unless such needs are met, closure is impossible.

In the aftermath of crime, victims' needs form the starting point for restorative justice. But one must not neglect offender and community needs.

A Matter of Accountability

Needs and responsibilities—it's a matter of accountability. When harm is done, offenders need to be accountable, and in ways that represent natural consequences of their actions. This accountability means understanding and acknowledging the harm and taking steps to make things right.

There is a third, intermediate dimension of account-ability by offenders: to share in the responsibility for deciding what needs to be done. Judge Challeen speaks of responsible sentencing.[16]

Since offenders' behavior often reflects irresponsibil-ity, simply to tell them what is going to happen lets them off the hook, encouraging further irresponsibility. In his court, therefore, he tells offenders the dimen-sions they must address. Then he tells them to come back with a proposal on how they expect to meet these requirements and how the sentence will be monitored and enforced. VORP works at this by having offenders negotiate and agree to restitution.

In a new "juvenile reparations" experiment operated by the Center for Community Justice here in Indiana, young offenders must come to our program before the "sentence" is decided. There they are encouraged to understand that their behavior does harm (1) to the victim, (2) to the community, and (3) to themselves. The staff works with them to help them propose a "sentence" which addresses all three. Through VORP, for example, they may learn of victims' needs and make restitution. Through community service they may seek to repay the community. Through tutoring, art therapy, or other activities they will address some of their own needs. It is not yet clear how successful this experi-ment will be, but the point is this: accountability should empower and encourage responsibility. And it should take seriously all three levels of obligation: vic-tim, community, and offender.

---

16. Dennis A. Challeen, *Making It Right: A Common Sense Approach to Crime* (Aberdeen, South Dakota: Mielius and Peterson Publishing, 1986).

Offenders must be held accountable, but so too must society. Society must be accountable to victims, helping to identify and meet their needs. Likewise, the larger community must attend to the needs of offenders, seeking not simply to restore but to transform. Accountability is multidimensional and transformational.

Understandings of Accountability

Retributive Lens	*Restorative Lens*
Wrongs create guilt	Wrongs create liabilities and obligations
Guilt absolute, either/or	Degrees of responsibility
Guilt indelible	Guilt removable through repentance and reparation
Debt is abstract	Debt is concrete
Debt paid by taking punishment	Debt paid by making right
"Debt" owed to society in the abstract	Debt owed to victim first
Accountability as taking one's "medicine"	Accountability as taking responsibility
Assumes behavior chosen freely	Recognizes difference between potential and actual realization of human freedom

| Free will or social determinism | Recognizes role of social context as choices without denying personal responsibility |

The Process Must Empower and Inform

Judges and lawyers often assume that what people want most is to win their cases. But recent studies show that the process matters a great deal, and that the criminal justice process often does not feel much like justice. Not only *what happens* but also *how it is decided* is important.[17]

Justice has to be lived, not simply done by others and reported to us. When someone simply informs us that justice has been done and that we should now go home (as victims) or to jail (as offenders), we do not experience that as justice. Justice which is actually lived, experienced, may not always be pleasant. But we will know that it has happened because we have lived it rather than having it done for us. Not simply justice, but the *experience* of justice must occur.

The first step in restorative justice is to meet immediate needs, particularly those of the victim. Following that, restorative justice should seek to identify larger needs and obligations. In identifying these needs and obligations, the process should, insofar as possible, put power and responsibility in the hands of those directly involved: the victim and offender. It should also leave room for community involvement. Second, it should address the victim-offender relationship by facilitating interaction and the exchange of information

---

17. See "Mediation," June 1988; and Martin Wright, *Making Good: Prisons, Punishment and Beyond* (London: Burnett Books, 1982), pp. 246ff.

about the events, about each other, and about each other's needs. Third, it should focus on problem-solving, addressing not only present needs but future intentions.

I have already spoken of the importance of participation for both victim and offender. For victims, disempowerment is a core element of the violation. Empowerment is crucial to recovery and justice. For offenders, irresponsibility and a sense of disempowerment may have been some of the bricks on the road to the offense. Only by participating in the "solution" can they move toward responsibility and closure.

The community has a role to play here too. Part of the tragedy of modern society is our tendency to turn over our problems to experts. That is our tendency with regard to health, education, and child-raising. And it certainly applies to the harms and conflicts we call crime. In doing that, we lose the power and ability to solve our own problems. Even worse, we give up opportunities to learn and grow from these situations. Restorative responses must recognize that the community has a role to play in the search for justice.

An important part of justice is the exchange of information—about each other, about the facts of the offense, about needs. Victims want answers to their questions about what happened, why it happened, and who did this thing. Offenders need to understand what they have done and to whom. Faces should take the place of stereotypes. Misattributions need to be challenged. The exchange of such information is crucial, and ideally it can occur through direct interaction. In that context, the question of what to do about what has happened in the past and what is to happen in the future can be addressed. Such outcomes need to be registered in the form of agreements and settlements which are measurable and monitored.

Mediation between victim and offender is one approach to justice which meets these criteria. Victim-offender mediation empowers participants, challenges misattributions, provides for an exchange of information, and encourages actions aimed at making right. Through the use of community mediators, it provides for community participation. Mediation is fully compatible with a restorative approach to justice.

Mediation assumes certain preconditions, however. Safety must be assured. Participants must receive the emotional support which they need and must be willing to participate. Trained mediators are essential. The timing must be right.

When such preconditions are met, mediation must be conducted appropriately and must address key issues. Mark Umbreit has pointed to the importance of an "empowering" style of mediation rather than one in which the mediator imposes his or her agenda and personality, either directly or through manipulation.[18]

One must not bypass the exchange of information and expression of feelings on the road to agreements. Ron Claassen teaches his VORP mediators that, for mediation to be complete, three questions must be satisfactorily answered:

First, has the injustice been recognized and acknowledged? Has the offender owned up to and accepted responsibility for his acts? Have victims' questions been answered? Has the offender had a chance to explain what has been going on in his life?

Second, has there been agreement on what needs to be done to restore equity as far as possible?

Third, have future intentions been addressed? Does

---

18. Mark Umbreit, *Victim Understanding of Fairness: Burglary Victims in Victim Offender Mediation* (Minneapolis: Minnesota Citizens Council on Crime and Justice, 1988), pp. 25ff.

the offender plan to do it again? Is the victim feeling safe? Is there provision for follow-up and for the monitoring of agreements?

In biblical language, Claassen summaries the three categories as confession, restitution, and repentance.[19]

But mediation is not always appropriate. The fear may be too great, even with support and assurances of safety. Power imbalances between parties may be too pronounced and impossible to overcome. The victim or the offender may be unwilling. The offense may be too heinous or the suffering too severe. One of the parties may be emotionally unstable. Direct contact between victim and offender can be extremely helpful, but justice cannot depend only on such direct interaction.

There are, in such cases, a variety of other ways to proceed which keep interaction and exchange of information in focus. The use of surrogate victims, pioneered by programs in Canada and England, is one example. Here offenders meet with victims other than their own as a step toward assuming responsibility and sharing information. This can be particularly helpful in emotionally-charged situations such as sexual offenses or where cases remain unsolved.[20]

Most sexual abuse therapy treats victims and offenders separately, in isolation. It provides little recognition or ways to work at the abuse of trust involved in the offense. It offers few avenues for closure. Little attention is given to how the events of the offense are perceived or to misattributions about the event or the individuals.

---

19. Claassen and Zehr, *VORP Organizing*, pp. 24-25.

20. See, for example, Gilles Launay and Peter Murray, "Victim/Offender Groups," *Mediation and Criminal Justice*, ed. Wright and Galaway, pp. 113-131.

"Victim-sensitive sex offender therapy" developed by therapist Walter Berea is different.[21] This therapeutic approach has three stages. The first is the "communication switchboard" stage. Here the therapist makes contact with the probation officer, previous therapists, and, perhaps most unusually, with the victim. Contact with the victim provides more complete information about the events, lets the victim know that the offender is in therapy, and allows the therapist to inquire whether the victim's needs are being met.

In the second stage of therapy misattributions about the victim are challenged. The offender is helped to acknowledge responsibility and to understand the consequences of his behavior. During this time, he writes a letter of apology to the victim. For the victim, this stage provides a time to make sure that he does not take fault or blame on himself.

The third and final stage of this therapy has a reconciliation focus. Options include actually receiving the letter of apology which the offender has written, a face-to-face meeting, or a "no-contact" contract with the offender for the future. The choice is the victim's. Such an approach takes seriously the harm and the interpersonal dimensions of the offense as well as the needs of both victim and offender.

"Genesee justice—crafted with pride in New York State." So reads the logo of a program operated by the sheriff's department in Batavia, New York. Concerned about overuse of the jail and about victims' needs, this program was designed specifically for cases of serious violence: manslaughter, assault, and homicide. When

21. Walter H. Bera, "A Three Stage Sex Offender/Victim Reconciliation Model with a Systemic and Attributional Analysis." Unpublished paper prepared for the Task Force on Restorative Justice, October 30 through November 2, 1986, Guelph, Ontario.

such an offense occurs, immediate and intensive aid is offered to victims and survivors. The support offered is holistic. It concentrates not simply on their legal needs, but on emotional and spiritual needs.

Staff persons walk through the victimization experience with victims. In the process they help them in providing full information to the "system" about their experience. During that process, victims are allowed some involvement in decisions such as bail and even sentencing, for example through a victim-offender encounter. Given all that support and participation, victims' wishes often turn out to be surprisingly creative and redemptive. At minimum, their needs are addressed and the various dimensions of the harm are recognized.

The ideals of direct victim-offender interaction and empowerment cannot always be fully attained. Some third-party decisions are inescapable. Cases with important implications for the community cannot simply be left up to victim and offender. There must also be some sort of community oversight. But these cases need not set the norm for how we view and respond to crime. Even in such cases, we need to keep before us a vision of what crime really is and what really should happen.

Justice Involves Rituals

Our legal system makes much of ritual. Indeed, trials are to a large extent ritual, drama, theater. But we usually ignore the most important needs for ritual.

One of these points of need is when an offense has occurred. This is where the ritual of lament, stated so eloquently in the Psalms, is appropriate. "Genesee justice" has recognized this need by facilitating religious services of lament and healing for those who are interested.

But as justice is done—whether complete or approximate—we also need rituals of closure. Louk Hulsman has called these "rituals of reordering." They may be important for both victim and offender.

Such rituals provide an arena in which the church could play a particularly important role.

Is There a Place for Punishment?

I have argued that punishment should not be the focus of justice. But is there room in a restorative concept for some forms of punishment? Certainly options such as restitution will be understood by some as punishment, albeit a more deserved and logical punishment. In one major study of VORP, for example, offenders described their outcomes as punishment but viewed them more positively than traditional punishment. Perhaps punitive language arose due to a lack of alternate terminology (although some did use the language of "making right" to describe justice). However, accepting responsibility is painful and will of necessity be understood in part as punishment. Similarly, isolation of those who are dangerous, even under the best of conditions, is painful.

The real question, then, is not whether persons will experience some elements of restorative justice as punishment, but whether punishment *intended as punishment* has a place. Christie has argued that if pain—intended as pain—is used, it should at least be used without an ulterior purpose.[22]

Pain should be applied simply as punishment, not as a way of reaching some other goal such as rehabilitation or social control. To apply pain with other utilitarian purposes is to be dishonest and to use people as

---

22. See works previously cited.

commodities. He makes the analogy with sorrow. When we mourn a death, we mourn for the sake of mourning, not for some other purpose. Christie also urges that we inflict pain only under conditions which will reduce the level of pain-infliction.

Perhaps punishment cannot be eliminated entirely from a restorative approach, but it should not be normative and its uses and purposes should be carefully prescribed. The biblical example suggests that the goal, nature, and context of punishment is critical. In the biblical context, for example, punishment usually is not the end. It aims at liberating and creating shalom. Biblical justice is administered in a context of love. Possibilities for forgiveness and reconciliation are the light at the end of the tunnel. Punishment is limited, while love is unlimited. Redeeming love, not punishment, is the primary human responsibility.

When we as a society punish, we must do so in a context that is just and deserving. Punishment must be viewed as fair and legitimate, Ignatieff notes, because we cannot experience justice unless it provides a framework of meanings that make sense of experience. For punishment to seem fair, outcome and process need to relate to the original wrong. However, the societal context must also be viewed as fair, and this raises larger questions of social, economic, and political justice.

If there is room for punishment in a restorative approach, its place would not be central. It would need to be applied under conditions which controlled and reduced the level of pain and in a context where restoration and healing are the goals. Perhaps there are possibilities for "restorative punishment." Having said that, however, I hasten to add that possibilities for destructive punishment are much more plentiful.

Two Lenses

Earlier I summarized briefly the retributive and restorative lenses. These two perspectives can be formulated in somewhat longer form. According to retributive justice, (1) crime violates the state and its laws; (2) justice focuses on establishing guilt (3) so that doses of pain can be measured out; (4) justice is sought through a conflict between adversaries (5) in which offender is pitted against state; (6) rules and intentions outweigh outcomes. One side wins and the other loses.

According to restorative justice, (1) crime violates people and relationships; (2) justice aims to identify needs and obligations (3) so that things can be made right; (4) justice encourages dialogue and mutual agreement, (5) gives victims and offenders central roles, and (6) is judged by the extent to which responsibilities are assumed, needs are met, and healing (of individuals and relationships) is encouraged.

Justice which seeks first to meet needs and to make right looks quite different from justice which has blame and pain at its core. The following chart attempts to contrast some characteristics and implications of the two concepts of justice.

Understandings of Justice

Retributive Lens	*Restorative Lens*
Blame-fixing central	Problem-solving central
Focus on past	Focus on future
Needs secondary	Needs primary

Battle model; adversarial	Dialogue normative
Emphasizes differences	Searches for commonalities
Imposition of pain considered normative	Restoration and reparation considered normative
One social injury added to another	Emphasis on repair of social injuries
Harm by offender balanced by harm to offender	Harm by offender balanced by making right
Focus on offender; victim ignored	Victims' needs central
State and offender are key elements	Victim and offender are key elements
Victims lack information	Information provided to victims
Restitution rare	Restitution normal
Victims' "truth" secondary	Victims given chance to "tell their truth"
Victims' suffering ignored	Victims' suffering lamented and acknowledged
Action from state to offender; offender passive	Offender given role in solution
State monopoly on response to wrongdoing	Victim, offender, and community roles recognized

Offender has no responsibility for resolution	Offender has responsibility in resolution
Outcomes encourage offender irresponsibility	Responsible behavior encouraged
Rituals of personal denunciation and exclusion	Rituals of lament and reordering
Offender denounced	Harmful act denounced
Offender's ties to community weakened	Offender's integration into community increased
Offender seen in fragments, offense being definitional	Offender viewed holistically
Sense of balance through retribution	Sense of balance through restitution
Balance righted by lowering offender	Balance righted by raising both victim and offender
Justice tested by intent and process	Justice tested by its "fruits"
Justice as right rules	Justice as right relationships
Victim-offender relationships ignored	Victim-offender relationships central
Process alienates	Process aims at reconciliation

Response based on offender's past behavior	Response based on consequences of offender's behavior
Repentance and forgiveness discouraged	Repentance and forgiveness encouraged
Proxy professions are the key actors	Victim and offender central; professional help available
Competitive, individualistic values encouraged	Mutuality and cooperation encouraged
Ignores social, economic, and moral context of behavior	Total context relevant
Assumes win-lose outcomes	Makes possible win-win outcomes

Retributive justice, restorative justice. The world looks quite differently through these two lenses. Retributive justice, we have. It may not do what needs to be done, or even what its practitioners claim it does, but it "works" in the sense that we know how to carry it out. What about the more elusive perspective that I've called restorative justice? Where do we go from here?

CHAPTER 11

Where to from Here?

How will we go about fully implementing a restorative system? It is fun to speculate.

System Possibilities

Some have urged that we "civilize" the law.[1]

Unlike criminal law, civil law defines wrongs in terms of injuries and liabilities rather than guilt. Outcomes, therefore, focus on settlement and restitution rather than punishment. They allow for degrees of responsibility without defining them in win/lose terms. Since the state is not the victim, the actual participants remain center stage, retaining significant power and responsibility in the process. Because outcomes are not primarily punitive, procedural safeguards are of less concern and the relevant facts are less circumscribed. What if we were to modify civil procedures to ensure certain safeguards? What if we made sure that victims had advocates in the process, allowing for third-party decisions when we could not reach agreements or when questions of danger were involved? What if we

---

1. Cf. Martin Wright, *Making Good* (London: Burnett Books, 1982), pp. 249-250.

removed cases from criminal procedures and processed them through a modified civil procedure?

The application of criminal law is what triggers the retributive paradigm. Yet criminal law is a relatively new addition to Western society and operates under assumptions that are in many ways at variance with the rest of life. The existing structure of civil law might provide an alternative framework for a concept of justice which avoided some of these assumptions.

Perhaps we should not dream of dismantling the retributive system but develop a parallel system with choices about which to use. Herman Bianchi has argued that the existence of two parallel tracks—state justice and church justice—in the medieval period was in some ways a good thing. The existence of two tracks provided choices for participants in certain cases. Moreover, each track served as a conscience and check on the other.

Development of a separate justice track has been the strategy of the Community Boards in San Francisco. These programs have been developing neighborhood-based structures for resolving disputes outside "the system." The programs train people from the community to serve as case workers and as mediators and place a high value on community education and empowerment. Their mediation processes serve as an alternative to civil or criminal courts. Indeed, they refuse to take on a case while it is in the legal process. The programs are a means of educating and empowering the community to solve its own problems.

The Community Boards and other dispute-resolution programs have shown much promise. They represent one way of actually implementing a problem-solving, community-oriented vision of justice. Yet such forms of "informal justice" have come under increasing attack in recent years.[2]

Various warnings are sounded. Outcomes may have no uniformity and thus contradict a basic sense of fairness. Informal justice may be reserved primarily for the poor and the powerless, denying them access to other forms of justice. Victims may be given too much power. In the end, the state and the formal justice system may actually receive more, not less, power and legitimation. The dispute resolution movement is being encouraged to consider its assumptions and goals carefully.

The Japanese model is particularly interesting in this context. John O. Haley, a specialist in Japanese law, reports that a unique two-track judicial system operates there.[3]

Separate formal and informal tracks operate parallel to one another, but with considerable dependence upon and interaction between them. A common pattern is for serious cases to begin in one but be transferred to the other.

One track is a Western-style, formal criminal system with many familiar characteristics. The process focuses on guilt and punishment. It is governed by formal rules and is operated by professionals such as public prosecutors. This track is used for many crimes. Yet few cases proceed all the way through the system, ending

---

2. See Roger Matthews, ed., *Informal Justice?* (London: Sage Publications, 1988).

3. I have drawn upon an unpublished paper, "Mediation and Criminal Justice: The Japanese Model—Confession, Repentance, and Absolution," presented to the CLE Seminar "Creative Justice Through Mediation" in Seattle, Washington, on October 29, 1988. See also John O. Haley, "Confession, Repentance and Absolution," in *Mediation and Criminal Justice*, eds. Martin Wright and Burt Galaway (London: Sage Publications, 1989), pp. 195-211.

in long imprisonment or other serious legal penalties. Cases are constantly shunted aside. To an outsider, the overall system seems remarkably lenient.

This apparent leniency and the lack of long-term involvement by the formal legal system is the result of a second, less formal, track for which there is no Western parallel. Haley summarizes it like this:

> A pattern of confession, repentance, and absolution dominates each stage of law enforcement in Japan. The players in the process include not only the authorities in new roles but also the offender and the victim. From the initial police interrogation through the final judicial hearing on sentencing, the vast majority of those accused of criminal offenses confess, display repentance, negotiate for their victims' pardon and submit to the mercy of the authorities. In return, they are treated with extraordinary leniency; they gain at least the prospect of institution[al] absolution by being dropped from the formal process altogether.

Cases are moved out of the formal legal system at each stage of the process. Only a fraction enter prosecution and an even smaller fraction are fully prosecuted. A smaller minority are incarcerated and few serve more than one year. This does not mean, however, that Japanese offenders are not convicted. In fact, conviction rates in Japan stand at about 99.5 percent!

A variety of factors influence decisions to shunt cases from the formal process or to impose nonpunitive sentences. Some of these considerations are familiar to Westerners, such as the seriousness of the offense and the nature of the offender. Added to this, however, are some unique variables: the willingness of the offender to acknowledge guilt, to express remorse and make compensation to the victim, and the victim's willingness to receive compensation and to pardon.

Conviction rates are high in Japan largely because offenders are willing to confess and take responsibility. The roots of this willingness are in part cultural, of course. In part, however, it is due to the understanding that, if they do, the outcome is likely to focus on compensation and correction more than punishment. Where the complex, punitive legal system in Western society discourages confession, the Japanese system appears to make it normative.

Victims have an important role to play in this process. Restitution for losses is expected. And they have a voice in the authorities' decisions to report, prosecute, or sentence the offender. Yet they do not control the process, nor do they assume the role of adversary or prosecutor.

Westerners are surprised at authorities' willingness to divert cases from the formal legal system. This is only because of our assumption that the formal process is primary and that its main focus is to establish guilt and apply punishment. The basic aim of the criminal process in Japan is to correct, and this governs authorities' decisions.

> Thus [the authorities'] roles are not confined to the formal tasks of apprehending, prosecuting and adjudicating. Rather, once personally convinced that a suspect is an offender, their concerns for evidentiary proof of guilt shifts to a concern over the suspect's attitude and prospects for rehabilitation and reintegration into society, including acceptance of authority. Leniency is considered an appropriate response if the correctional process has begun.

Haley says that typical of the Japanese pattern of responding to crime are

> acknowledgment of guilt, expression of remorse including direct negotiation with the victim for restitution and par-

don as preconditions for lenient treatment, and sparing resort to long-term imprisonment.

Westerners assume that such a "lenient" response would fail to deter crime. Haley, however, concludes that this pattern of response is in fact partly responsible for low crime rates in Japan.

Haley marvels that the Japanese have institutionalized the concepts of repentance and forgiveness while the West has not. The imperative to repent and forgive is at least as strong in the Judeo-Christian tradition as it is in the Japanese. Yet the West has

> failed to develop institutional props for implementing such moral commands. Instead, the legal institutions and processes of Western law both reflect and reinforce societal demands for retribution and revenge.

While the Japanese pattern is obviously tied to Japanese culture, Haley believes that we have much to learn from that example. It suggests intriguing possibilities for linking formal and informal, adversarial and nonadversarial, systems. The Japanese model suggests a place for the formal machinery of justice and for the state while leaving space for restoration and giving victim and offender an enlarged role. While the West cannot simply imitate this model, it suggests that justice might be both personal and formal. Jerome Auerbach has worried about the dangers of law without justice but especially of injustice without law. The Japanese pattern gives hope that these are not the only two possibilities.

The possibilities are intriguing. However, I must admit to considerable skepticism about blueprints for system-wide implementation, certainly at this stage. I was relieved to have Kay Harris, at a recent workshop on restorative justice, urge us to continue to develop the vision and to resist pressures for "premature practicality."[4]

Much conceptual work remains to be done. In the previous chapter I noted that restorative justice is not yet a paradigm. Many issues remain undeveloped or unanswered. *Community* is an elusive, oft-abused term. What does it mean and how could it be given reality in a restorative approach? What is the proper role of the state?

I have emphasized the responsibilities *of* offenders, but what about responsibilities *to* offenders? What do we do with the "dangerous few"? Do we incarcerate? If so, how do we make these decisions? Is there a place for punishment? How does the idea of restorative justice in the area of crime mesh with larger questions of social, economic, and political justice? The biblical material assumes a close connection, but what does this mean in practical terms today?

Furthermore, to what extent does my formulation reflect a white, middle-class, male, North American perspective? Kay Harris' work on a feminist concept of justice points in some of the same directions, but not entirely.[5] The idea of restorative justice needs to be tested against the perspectives of a variety of cultures, traditions, and experiences.

Even if one could present restorative justice as a full-fledged paradigm, however, I must admit that I would remain wary about system-wide implementation.

---

4. See M. Kay Harris, "Alternative Visions in the Context of Contemporary Realities," in *Justice: The Restorative Vision*, Issue No. 7 of *New Perspectives on Crime and Justice: Occasional Papers* (Akron, Pennsylvania: Mennonite Central Committee, 1989), pp. 31-40.

5. See "Moving into the New Millennium: Toward a Feminist Vision of Justice," *Prison Journal*, 67, No. 2 (Fall-Winter, 1987), pp. 27-38.

One of the deficiencies of Kuhn's theory of paradigm change is that it treats paradigm change as an intellectual activity, neglecting the politics and institutional dynamics of paradigm shifts. Political and institutional interests and processes certainly affect whether shifts occur and what form they finally take. The retributive paradigm is closely tied to the interests and functions of the modern state. That will have considerable impact on whether the paradigm changes and, if it does, what shape it takes.

The history of change in the area of law and justice is not a hopeful one. Efforts at change have often been co-opted and diverted from their original visions, sometimes in perverse and harmful ways. The origin of prisons is a case at point, and must stand as a constant reminder and warning to those of us who think about change. Perhaps such "improvements" have gone wrong because they did not question fundamental assumptions, as I suggested earlier. But the issues are more complex than that.

Sometimes so-called alternatives have used new language to clothe ideas that were not new.[6] Often ideas have hidden implications which take time to emerge. And a variety of pressures—internal and external—tend to sidetrack such efforts from their original directions. Sometimes they end up reshaping them so they serve interests and goals quite different from those projected.

Before we dream too grandly, then, we have an obligation to think through implications carefully. We must be as literate as possible about the dynamics of change and we must project how our dreams can go wrong.

---

6. Matthews, *Informal Justice?* p. 102.

In the Meantime

While we contemplate larger possibilities, we must also pursue interim goals and activities. There are things that we can and must do here and now, in the meantime.

We must continue to dialogue, to "palaver"[7] with those who are sympathetic and those who are not. We must test, explore, and develop our vision.

We must also become justice farmers, planting our experimental and demonstration plots. We must plant more VORPs, for example, and test new forms and applications of VORP. We should offer new services to victims which operate from a restorative framework. These include all-important rituals which will show that we as a community stand with them in their suffering, in denouncing the wrong, and in seeking healing. Likewise, we need to offer new services to offenders and their families. Through it all, we need to explore alternatives to punishment which offer possibilities for accountability, repair, and empowerment.

Through VORP, we know something about restorative approaches to property crime. Now it is time to further apply the "tough case" test. What about murder? What about spouse and child abuse? Rape? What are the possibilities and what are the limits? What procedures work and which do not? What safeguards do we need?

---

7. We are using this term (from the Portuguese *palavra*, to talk) for our discussions at the suggestion of Herman Bianchi. Recently Russ Immarigeon of the Maine Council of Churches pointed out that, according to *The American Heritage Dictionary*, it is defined as "idle chatter," or "talk intended to charm or beguile," or "a parley between European explorers and representatives of the local populations, especially in Africa." Are we up to "idle chatter?" he asks. And why "especially in Africa"?

The dictionary shows another, more neutral level of meaning having to do with discussion and debate, but perhaps these other connotations need to be kept in mind!

Discussion and testing of such issues has begun, but much work remains. This will require creativity, risk-taking, and dreaming as well as realism, hard work, and caution. It will require cooperation between theoreticians and practitioners, between "experts" and lay-persons. The involvement of former victims and offenders will be essential.

As we and others pursue our "alternatives," we will have to test constantly whether they really are alternatives. Do they in fact reflect alternative values? Or are they simply alternative technologies? Are they consistent with a restorative focus? Do they move us in that direction?

We must develop interim strategies and approaches, but we must be thoughtful about where they can take us. At minimum, we should ask the following of our efforts: Do they encourage or discourage punishment values? Can they be used to construct new modes of control or punishment? Will they provide a reservoir of experience, serving as experimental or demonstration "plots"? Do they take incorporate key elements of a restorative vision?

What are those "key elements" of a restorative vision? Perhaps we could begin to develop a restorative yardstick against which to measure our efforts. I have attempted a fuller listing in the Appendix, but primary would be questions such as these: Does the program or outcome seek to make right the harm to the victim? Does it address the needs of the offender? Does it take into account community needs and responsibilities? Does it address the victim-offender relationship? Does it encourage offender responsibility? Are victim and offender encouraged to participate in both process and outcome?

New Within the Old

Meanwhile, church has a key role to play. Old Testament scholar Millard Lind has reminded us that biblical justice stood then as now—in marked contrast to state justice. He poses an important question: "How do Christians relate this new, transformed model of justice to the justice systems of this world?" What is the Christian community's responsibility?

Lind looks at four of the church's responses over the centuries. The first is a strategy of withdrawal. At points the church has tried to insulate itself from the world. The withdrawal strategy is a strategy of unfaithfulness, however, because it ignores the "aggressive" character of God's justice, which is to be shared with others. A second response is the Constantinian one, a strategy of capitulation. This has been the predominant response of the church, which has largely adopted the assumptions of the secular world. A third strategy was that adopted by the Enlightenment, a strategy which denies the tension between models of justice.

Christ's strategy, however, presented a fourth option: to create the new in the midst of the old. In *Easy Essays*, Peter Maurin captured this spirit nicely in his words about the Catholic Worker.

> The Catholic Worker believes in creating a new society within the shell of the old with the philosophy of the new, which is not a new philosophy but a very old philosophy, a philosophy so old that it looks like new.

Christ's strategy was to create a new society (the church) with new operating principles and assumptions which would operate in the midst of—and serve as an example and challenge to—the old.[8]

---

8. See John H. Yoder, *The Original Revolution* (Scottdale, Pennsylvania: Herald Press, 1971).

Part of the answer to Lind's question, then, is to get our own act together. Too often within the church, we have ignored the victims and have responded to wrongdoing with a retributive lens borrowed from the larger society. The apostle Paul warned that Christians should avoid taking their disputes to state courts which operate under inappropriate assumptions. His point was not merely negative, however. He assumed that the church should develop its own alternative structures to implement covenant justice. Surely we must reexamine the lenses we use for dealing with harm and conflict within the church and create new structures which incorporate a restorative understanding. In this way, the church can provide a model to others.[9]

When we operate outside the church's framework, we need to take our restorative lens with us, allowing it to shape and inform what we do. The church must also lead the way in setting up alternative structures within the old framework. We must take the lead in planting plots which can serve as tests and models.

If we are ever to develop an alternative to retributive justice which is in fact a genuine paradigm, we will have to move beyond theory to a new grammar and a new "physics." That is, we need a new language but also a set of principles and procedures for implementation which can "make sense" of the paradigm. The church has a special responsibility in this process.

If Nothing Else

Retributive justice is deeply embedded in our political institutions and our psyche. Perhaps it is too much

---

9. For material on resolving conflicts within the church, contact Mennonite Conciliation Service, Box M, Akron, PA 17501.

to hope for that to change in fundamental ways. Yet we must recognize the importance of the paradigms we use and free ourselves to question these paradigms. We can also begin to use a new lens to inform and shape what we decide is worth doing. And we can begin to use another lens in the areas of our lives where we do have some control: within our families, our churches, our daily lives.

If restorative justice is not a paradigm, perhaps it nevertheless can serve as what one writer has called a "sensitizing theory."[10] Perhaps it can at least cause us to think carefully before we impose pain.

Observers have sought to understand why Holland has had such low incarceration rates since World War II. One recent study has concluded that the reluctance to impose prison there is less the result of a particular philosophy of sentencing than the result of a "bad conscience" about prison.[11]

The experience of imprisonment at the hands of the Nazis and a law-school curriculum that questioned imprisonment shaped a whole generation of jurists. The result has been a hesitation to impose pain in the form of imprisonment. If nothing else, discussions about our lenses can contribute to a milieu in which the infliction of pain is a last resort, a statement of failure, rather than the hub of justice.

---

10. Sebastian Scheerer, "Towards Abolitionism," *Contemporary Crises: Law, Crime and Social Policy*, 10, No. 1 (1986), p. 9.

11. Willem De Haan, "Abolitionism and the Politics of 'Bad Conscience,' " *The Howard Journal of Criminal Justice*, 26, No. 1 (February 1987), pp. 15-32.

Afterword

What I have written here may sound impossibly visionary and unrealistic. So the abolition of slavery once sounded. In fact, much of what we today assume as common sense was once considered utopian. Lenses do change.

Still, I must confess that for me personally, in my own life, it sometimes does feel utopian. Confronted with my own anger, my own tendencies to blame, my own reluctance to dialogue, my own distaste for conflict, I have at times been afraid to write this book.

Yet I believe in ideals. Much of the time we fall short of them but they remain a beacon, something toward which to aim, something against which to test our actions. They point a direction. Only with a sense of direction can we know when we are off the path.

The place to begin experiencing restoration is not from the top but from the bottom, in our own homes and communities. I continue to have faith that the community of God's people can lead in this direction. Certainly we will often fail, as those in the biblical record did. But just as certainly God will forgive and restore us.

I have confessed that restorative justice is in part an

ideal, but that raises another concern. I worry that because of this confession, the reader will not take this vision seriously. I recall the preface to Copernicus' book—not to imply that my own is in the same class, but for the lesson that we can learn from it.

Copernicus' book revolutionized the way we think about the cosmos itself. It was a key element in the paradigm shift known as the scientific revolution. Yet a century passed before people took it seriously.

People did not take Copernicus' book seriously at first—in part because it went counter to the common sense of the era. However, its preface may have encouraged its neglect. In that preface, the writer Oreander said, in effect, "Look, reader, what an interesting book. It deserves to be read. But remember, it's just an idea, a model, a vision. It is not necessarily reality." That comment may have made this radical book more palatable to its enemies, but it let the reader off the hook by suggesting that the Copernican paradigm was just an imaginary model. I fear that I may do so as well.

My hope is that you will understand this as a vision —a vision that is less an elusive mirage than it is an indistinct destination on a necessarily long and circuitous road.

A Restorative Justice Yardstick

1. Do victims experience justice?
    - Are there sufficient opportunities for them to tell their truth to relevant listeners?
    - Are they receiving needed compensation or restitution?
    - Is the injustice adequately acknowledged?
    - Are they sufficiently protected against further violation?
    - Does the outcome adequately reflect the severity of the offense?
    - Are they receiving adequate information about the event, the offender, and the process?
    - Do they have a voice in the process?
    - Is the experience of justice adequately public?
    - Do they have adequate support from others?
    - Are their families receiving adequate assistance and support?
    - Are other needs—material, psychological, spiritual—being addressed?

2. Do offenders experience justice?
    - Are they encouraged to understand and take responsibility for what they have done?
    - Are misattributions challenged?

- Are they provided encouragement and opportunity to make things right?
- Are they given the opportunity to participate in the process?
- Is there encouragement toward changed behavior (repentance)?
- Is there a mechanism for monitoring or verifying changes?
- Are their own needs being addressed?
- Are their families receiving support and assistance?

3. Is the victim-offender relationship addressed?
- Is there opportunity for a meeting, if appropriate—either direct or therapeutic?
- Is there opportunity and encouragement for an exchange of information—about the event, about one another?
- Are misattributions being challenged?

4. Are community concerns being taken into account?
- Is the process and outcome sufficiently public?
- Is community protection being addressed?
- Is there need for some restitution or symbolic action for the community?
- Is the community represented in some way in the process?

5. Is the future being addressed?
- Is there provision for solving the problems which led up to this event?
- Is there provision for solving problems caused by this event?
- Have future intentions been addressed?
- Is there provision for monitoring, verifying, and troubleshooting outcomes?

The Subversion of Visions

As reforming visions are made operational, they tend to be diverted (or subverted) from their original intents. Sometimes they end up serving purposes quite opposed to their original intent. This tendency is obvious in many areas, including—and some would argue, especially—in criminal justice. VORP too could become something quite different than what was envisioned. Indeed, some have argued that the process is well under way.

Over the years that I have been involved in some way with VORP, I have struggled to understand the forces which tend to distort our visions. Such distortion may be inevitable, but it can be minimized if we understand the dynamics of the process. The following is an attempt to catalog some of the sources of this diversion or subversion as I understand them. I've organized them under three categories.

Criminal Justice Interests

In VORP circles, a frequently discussed source of diversion has to do with the conflict between retributive and restorative goals. The criminal justice system is essentially retributive, seeking primarily to punish. VORP, however, claims to be concerned with restoration. Can those two goals coexist, or will the larger system pressure us to share its goals? If we speak language the system understands, the language of punishment, the punitive may come to overshadow the restorative. If we refuse to speak the language of punishment, chances are that we will remain marginal, nonessential for "minor" cases.

The criminal justice process creates diversionary pressures in other ways. Criminal justice is inherently offender-oriented. The event, the case, and the principal actors are all defined in terms of the offender. The victim has little legal standing. If we work alongside and get referrals from an offender-oriented system, can we retain equal and genuine justice for victims?

A third source of pressure from the criminal justice process has to do with its own self-interests. As I have noted before, the various parts of the "system" have their own interests and they tend to find ways to co-opt and control new concepts to fit these interests. In *Justice Without Law*, Jerome Auerbach has provided an anatomy of this process for conflict resolution processes in American history.

The Dynamics of Institutionalization

For ideas to become reality, institutions need to be created. The dynamics of those institutions themselves create diversionary pressures.

Administrative considerations become important. Administration requires measurements that are easily collected, tabulated, and processed. One can, in turn, use these measurements to justify the organization's existence. With VORP, for instance, it is tempting to measure our value by the number of cases handled and by "successful" outcomes.

Since reconciliation is hard to measure, we may come to emphasize restitution which is much easier to measure. We may put pressures on mediators to finish cases quickly to maintain volume, without regard to the quality of outcome. We could turn to professional mediators. Administrative goals and measurements can easily reshape the vision.

As this implies, subsistence questions are involved. This quickly takes us to the issue of funding and funding sources. To do our good things, we have to have money. As someone has said, programs tend to end up looking like their funding sources.

Another dimension to the "dynamics of institutionalization" has to do with the development of staff identities and career goals. As institutions develop, people begin to look to careers within them. And they begin to make decisions about themselves and about the program with career goals in mind. The effects of this are subtle but important.

All of us look to others around us for support, for peers. Where do those of us involved in VORP look for our peers? As we establish ourselves, we probably begin to look for peers within criminal justice circles. That has its strengths, but it also creates pressures to conform to the values and assumptions which operate within that system.

The hired staff and the values they hold are critical. Most analyses of the subversion of reform have focused on a gradual co-optation process. The process, however, is more fundamental and begins sooner. While leaders articulate a grand vision, the staff may come from traditional criminal justice jobs and hold traditional criminal justice values. Guided by a traditional perspective instead of an alternative paradigm, they tend to do things the traditional way. If not all share alternate values, it is hard to make a real difference.

As they develop, organizations move through various stages. These stages call forth certain types of leadership, each with its own strengths and weakness. This too affects the shape of a program.

The early stages of an organization require entrepreneurs. Usually a handful of people provide leadership. Among them are visionaries, risk-takers. Creativity must be high. Ideas have to be shaped and made workable. Resources have to be found and fit together in creative ways.

People with these entrepreneurial qualities bring considerable energy, enthusiasm, and creativity to their work. Often, however, they are not managers. At some point, therefore, it is important for leadership to become more managerial to cope with the realities of maintaining an organization and program. Managers, however, often are not visionaries. They may be preoccupied with the necessities of day-to-day operations and less concerned about long-term implications, program evaluation, and dreaming. They may not like to take risks. If programs move into the "managerial" stage without building in prophetic and visioning functions, another potential source of diversion is created.

Program Design and Operation

Programs often seek to meet a variety of goals. But good operation often requires only one primary goal. Moreover, goals may be contradictory.

We have found that true for the VORP here in Elkhart, and recent research in England suggests the same there. The goal of diverting people from jail sometimes conflicts with the goal of reconciliation, for example. Programs begun primarily to divert from jail may come to de-emphasize reconciliation and victim concerns.

As this suggests, it is easy to implement policies without examining their long-term implications, both practical and philosophical. A series of small, concrete steps, unexamined, may take us far off our path. And we may unawaringly lose our way.

Suggestions for Group Study

The following study questions and activity ideas are intended to provide help for those who wish to use this book in a group-study setting. Chapter 1 has no study questions since the vignette in that chapter merely forms the basis for the discussion in the following chapters.

Group leaders should select those questions and activity ideas that will be most fruitful for their particular learning situation. Although there are far more than an hour's worth of questions and activity ideas for each chapter, they are meant only as suggestions to facilitate group study of the book. Group leaders should feel free to devise other questions and other activity ideas.

Groups are encouraged to develop other creative suggestions on how to deal with criminals and other practical ideas for action on the local level. Please send these suggestions and other feedback on the book to:

Howard Zehr
Mennonite Central Committee U.S.
Office of Criminal Justice
107 West Lexington Ave.
Elkhart, IN 46516

Chapter 2
The Victim

Questions

1. Suppose you came home to find that your home had been broken into and vandalized. Valuable property, including several family heirlooms, are gone, and an ax was obviously used to get in. How would you feel? How would it affect you? What questions would you have? What would you need?

2. Have you known crime victims personally? Have you been victimized yourself? How did you react? How did you feel?

3. What do you believe should have happened in the "Vignette" case, from the victim's perspective?

4. In what ways does the experience of crime victims parallel that of other victims (e.g., illness, natural disasters)? What is different? (Note especially the section, "Why So Traumatic?")

5. Do you agree that anger is a natural part of healing and that its expression should be encouraged? How do you personally respond to someone who is hurt and angry?

6. Charlotte Hullinger lists four types of helper (see footnote 2). What are the strengths and weaknesses of each? Which are you? What can you do to be a "positive helper"?

7. Some argue that retribution is an inherent human need. They say if it is not fulfilled by government action, it will be taken on by individuals. Others argue that it is learned. Some argue that it represents a need that is better filled through other processes such as restitution and forgiveness. What do you think?

8. What are some of the ways we tend to blame victims? Why do we do so?

9. Discuss the six questions for healing (see "Why

So Traumatic?"). What will it take to answer each? Who can do it? Who can and should assist for each?

10. What rights and role should victims have in the justice process? What would be the advantages and disadvantages or dangers of this kind of involvement—for the victim, for the offender, for the system itself?

11. What about spouse abuse or incest? What is similar and what is different from crimes such as burglary or assault?

Activities

1. On a board or flipchart list a series of victim-related words such as these:

victim
burglary
court
justice
prosecutor
revenge
restitution

Go through the list, having people call out whatever associations or ideas come to mind for each word. Write these down. After the list is complete, analyze these associations together.

2. Develop a role play, providing details of a specific case. Divide into three-person groups, with a victim, a friend or service-provider (e.g., police officer), and an observer. Have the victim enact his or her part and the friend or service-provider respond.

3. Invite a victim or victim-assistance worker to talk about his or her experience. (Alternately, view one of the audiovisuals available from the resource offices listed.)

4. Outline the basic details of an actual case (if you do not have information locally, use one of the cases from Neiderback, *Invisible Wounds,* listed in the biblio-

graphy). Discuss what you think are the victim's basic needs. Who can and should provide what? What could you as an individual do? What could the church do? The "system"? The community?

5. Invite someone from the "system" to talk about the role of the victim in the legal process—preferably a victim advocate (victim assistance program, rape crisis center, etc.) or possibly a lawyer, prosecutor, or judge. What are the victim's rights? What is the victim's usual role? How is he or she usually treated? You might also invite a crime victim to share in this session.

Chapter 3
The Offender

Questions

1. What do you think of the outcome for the offender in the beginning "vignette" case? If you were asked to develop an alternate proposal, what would you propose?

2. What does the author suggest about concepts of self-worth and personal power and their relationships to offending? Do you agree? (See also chapter 4.)

3. What are the various nonprison sentences typically used in today's society (e.g., community service, probation, treatment, halfway houses, restitution)? What are the advantages and disadvantages of each? What does each attempt to accomplish? To what extent does each seek to punish?

4. What, if any, is the appropriate purpose and place of prison in our legal system?

5. What does the author include in the term *accountability*? How does this square with your own concept? Should accountability be a central goal of justice and, if so, how should it be obtained?

6. Is it helpful to view offenders as people who have themselves been violated? To what extent does their

behavior grow out of abuse at home or restricted educational and employment opportunities? How should this affect their responsibility? How does it affect society's responsibility?

Activities

1. As in the suggestions for chapter 2, list a series of words on the board. Have the group call out their associations. After they have run out of ideas, analyze their responses.

Suggested words:

offender
criminal
prison
judge
punishment
revenge
court

2. Invite a judge or probation officer who does presentence reports to talk about how sentencing recommendations and decisions are made.

3. Invite a therapist who works with offenders to discuss common "misattributions" and "exculpatory strategies"—stereotypes and rationalizations used to justify and rationalize wrongful behavior.

4. View and discuss one of the audiovisuals available from the resource programs listed in the appendix.

Chapter 4
Some Common Themes

Questions

1. What does repentance and forgiveness mean to you?

2. Is forgiveness compatible with the legal system? Is it an appropriate concern in relation to crime? If so, how can it be encouraged? What dangers do you see?

3. What does the author mean by "forgiveness is a gift; it should not be made into a burden"? Does this fit your understanding of forgiveness?

4. What is the role of repentance and forgiveness in the process of moving from victim to survivor? Can this recovery happen without forgiveness? How?

5. The author argues that certain preconditions facilitate forgiveness. What are they? Do you agree? Is this biblical?

6. Discuss ways the church could use "rituals of lament" and "rituals of reordering" (e.g., rituals of forgiveness and reconciliation) with victims and offenders.

7. What is the relationship between guilt and punishment? Does punishment relieve guilt (logically, emotionally, biblically)? Should it? What are other alternatives?

8. What are the requirements for punishment to be "just"?

9. What are the requirements for punishment to be "effective"? What would it mean for punishment to be "effective"?

10. The author suggests that wrongful behavior is often rooted in self-hate more fundamentally than in self-love. Is this true? If so, how does that affect our approaches to healing and rehabilitation?

11. What can we do as individuals, society, and the church to "demystify" crime?

Activities

1. Examine news clippings of crime coverage from a local paper. List and discuss ways news coverage of crime encourages fear as well as stereotypes and misconceptions about crime, victims, offenders, officials, and the justice process.

2. Invite a reporter who covers crime to talk to your group about how this news is obtained and reported.

3. Invite members of the group or people from outside (e.g., a victim or offender) to talk about how they understand and have experienced—or failed to experience—forgiveness.

Chapter 5
Retributive Justice

Questions

1. List and evaluate the six assumptions identified in this chapter. Are these in fact our assumptions? Are there others? Are they the "right" ones?

2. What is your understanding of guilt? What is the biblical understanding? What other understandings of guilt operate in various arenas of our society (e.g., social science, therapy, law)? What are the strengths and weaknesses of the various perspectives?

3. To what extent does the legal process encourage or discourage an understaning and acceptance of responsibility on the part of offenders?

4. Is our understanding of guilt and responsibility as individualistic as the author suggests? Is this a problem? What are the alternatives?

5. Is there a way to understand responsibility which can take into account both personal responsibility and the social, economic, and political context of behavior? Can this be incorporated into our legal system?

6. In what ways does our legal system encourage a "them" and "us" mentality? (And who are "them" and "us"?) What are the consequences?

7. Define *punishment.* Is the implied definition of *punishment* as "pain, intended as pain," adequate?

8. Is it really true that most people believe wrongdoing must be balanced by punishment? If so, is this a learned equation or is it rooted in human psychology? Is it biblical? Are there alternatives?

9. Does punishment satisfy victims? Offenders? What is your own experience with punishment?

10. What are some of the ways (including terminology) we try to hide the reality of punishment?

11. How do the following terms relate to one another: punishment, retribution, vengeance, revenge?

12. Examine your own tendencies and experiences with your friends, your spouse, or your children. When you feel wronged, is yours basically a "tit-for-tat" perspective, a "problem-solving" perspective, or do you take some other approach?

13. What does it mean that our system is "adversarial"? What are the implications?

14. Examine your own assumptions about wrongdoing. Do you tend to define it in terms of breaking rules or in terms of consequences and harm? What are the consequences of those two perspectives?

15. Did you realize before this that the state, not the individual, is the legal victim of a crime? What are some of the implications for you if you were (or have been) a victim?

Activities

1. Make up a case. Ask a variety of criminal justice officials (judges, probation officers, lawyers, prosecutors) to say what they think should be the sentence or outcome. Report back and compare the results.

2. Ask the group to take positions on a series of statements. Ask those who wish to register disagreement to stand at one end of the room, those registering agreement at the other, and those undecided to stand in the center. They will need to rearrange themselves after each statement. Pause to discuss the reasons for your opinions between each statement.

Sample statements (make your own):

a. The death penalty should be used for all murderers.

b. The death penalty should be used for the worst murderers only.

c. Spouse abuse should be declared and treated as crime.

d. People who commit crimes should pay by going to prison.

Chapter 6
Justice as Paradigm

Questions

1. What does the author mean by *paradigm*?

2. What are some of the paradigms we use to understand the world, not only in realms such as physics and psychology but in daily life (e.g., in family relationships, the workplace, etc.)?

3. How do those paradigms shape what we accept as relevant problems and solutions?

4. What is it about crime that makes us view and treat it differently from other wrongs and harms? Should we view and treat it differently? If so, where would we draw the line between them?

5. What are some of the ways civil law differs from criminal law? What decides where a situation will be treated as civil or criminal?

6. What nonlegal means of resolving harms and conflicts do we use in our everyday life and in society as a whole? Give examples from your own experience.

7. What signs, if any, are there that we may be on the verge of a shift in justice paradigms? (E.g., what are some of the signs of dysfunction or crisis?)

8. Evaluate current criminal justice reforms (e.g., victim assistance, intensive probation, private prisons, electronic monitoring, community service). To what ex-

tent do they point in new directions? To what extent are they simply patches in the paradigm?

Activities

Suppose two children get into a fight at school and one knocks a tooth from the other. This could be treated as a problem requiring punishment, a conflict needing resolution, or a damage requiring restitution. It could be seen as something to settle within the school, as a criminal case, or it could be taken to civil court. All these and other responses can and do occur in such situations.

Discuss what governs the response to such a situation. What are the likely consequences of each? Which is likely to be most satisfactory and why? How does the response chosen affect the eventual understanding of the original fight?

Chapter 7
Community Justice: The Historical Alternative

Questions

1. What have you heard or been taught about the way crime was handled in the past? How does this compare with the author's portrayal?

2. What are the differences between "private justice" and "public justice"? "state justice" and "community justice"? (It might be helpful to draw the state-community justice continuum that the author suggests.) How do the poles differ?

3. Which justice system would you prefer to live under—modern or premodern? Why? What would you like to see changed in the system you choose?

4. What were the three options for justice in the premodern world according to the author? What would you like to see changed in the system you choose? Why?

5. The author notes the importance of "moral vindication" when wrong has been committed. What does this mean? Is it important? What are some of the ways this has happened in the past? How does it happen today? How could it happen in an improved system?

6. In what ways has Christian theology served to underpin the emerging "retributive" understanding of crime?

7. In what ways does modern punishment try to reach the soul, as Michael Foucault puts it, and not just the body?

8. What has been positive and what has been negative about the legal revolution?

9. In what ways does punishment serve a symbolic role today?

Chapter 8
Covenant Justice: The
Biblical Alternative

Questions

1. The author argues that the law in the Old Testament had a different meaning and function than law today. What are some of the differences? What are the implications?

2. Test the basic tenets of your faith against the concept of shalom. Does it change anything if you try to base your thinking in a vision of shalom?

3. What has been your assumption in the past about the role and meaning of "an eye for an eye"? Has your understanding changed? If so, how?

4. What are some Old Testament assumptions about guilt? To what extent do we share those assumptions today?

5. Our understandings of biblical justice may ultimately rest on our images of God. For some, the image of God as a loving parent is predominant. Others see

God first of all as a stern judge. What other possibilities are there? What is your predominant image?

6. What is the relationship between shalom justice and "tit-for-tat" justice in the Old Testament? How does our concept of "tit-for-tat" or reciprocity change if it is rooted in shalom?

7. In what ways did the twin concepts of *shalom* and *covenant* make biblical law different from the law of the surrounding societies? That is, how do those concepts "transform" law and its application?

8. How does the "biblical yardstick" square with your own understandings? Are the comparisons with modern justice valid?

9. What would happen if we measured justice by its "fruits" (i.e., by the outcome, rather than by the process)? What are the possible benefits and dangers?

10. What happens to our understandings of the Ten Commandments and the Sermon on the Mount if we treat them as invitations and promises more than prohibitions and prescriptions? Does this seem an appropriate way to understand them?

11. If we take shalom seriously as a goal and vision, can we continue to treat *criminal* justice without addressing other justice issues? If not, what are the implications?

12. Modern justice is usually imaged as a blindfolded goddess holding a scales. What are the meanings of this image? In what ways is this a healthy image? In what ways might it be a dangerous image? What might be an appropriate image for restorative justice?

Activities

1. Note some biblical examples of vengeance. Now seek out examples of forgiveness and reconciliation. Which theme seems more important to you in the Old

Testament? In the New Testament? How do you understand the relationship between these two themes?

2. Read and discuss Psalm 103. What vision of justice emerges here? How does it relate to other, more retributive, themes in the Old Testament? (You may also wish to examine Leviticus 26 and Deuteronomy 4.)

3. Read the book of Hosea. Note and discuss the form in which God presents grievances here.

4. Outline a particular case taken from the newspaper. Examine what was done with it against the "biblical yardstick." Now, using that or some other biblical yardstick, discuss what might have been done with such a situation.

5. Examine various examples of biblical law. In particular, watch for the "therefore" pattern. What is the impact of this pattern on the thrust of that law?

Chapter 9 VORP:
An Experimental Plot

Questions

1. What are some potential benefits of the VORP approach? What are some potential problems?

2. If you were a victim (or offender) contemplating participation in VORP, what potential benefits might you see for yourself? What would be your worries? What would be the factors that might make you decide to participate or not?

3. If you were a victim (or offender) participating in VORP, what would you most want to happen at the meeting? What would you most want to see happen as an outcome of the meeting?

4. What should be the one primary goal for VORP? What other goals might be appropriate? Which would not?

5. If reconciliation should be a goal of VORP, what would that mean? How would it be measured?

6. How might the basic VORP approach be modified to use in "tough cases" (e.g., rape, murder, domestic violence)? Should it be used in such cases? What are the potential benefits and dangers?

7. Can you think of other ways a VORP approach might be used in our society (e.g., outside criminal justice)?

8. How can and should the church be involved in VORP? What are the possibilities and responsibilities of the church here? What form should this involvement take? (You may wish to use the handbook, *VORP Organizing: A Foundation in the Church,* available from Mennonite Central Committee. (Address is in the appendix.)

Activities

1. Role-play a victim-offender reconciliation meeting. Divide into groups of three or four, with people playing the parts of victim, offender, mediator, and possibly observer. (For role play suggestions, see *The Role Play Book* designed for use in mediation training. It is available from Mennonite Conciliation Service, whose address is in the appendix.)

2. View and discuss an audiovisual about VORP. Try the slide sets, "Crime: The Broken Community" and "Crime: Mediating the Conflict" or the video, "Going Straight." See the resource lists from MCC and the PACT Institute of Justice listed in the appendix.

3. If you are in a community which has a Victim Offender Reconciliation Program, invite a staff member, volunteer mediator, victim, or offender from the program to talk with your group.

Chapter 10
A Restorative Lens

Questions

1. What are the primary differences between the retributive and restorative "lenses"? List and evaluate the differences.

2. What would a satisfying "experience of justice" look like for a victim? For an offender?

3. Can "restorative justice" really provide a new lens or does it serve mainly as a corrective to the present system?

4. What happens if a restorative approach is implemented within a system and society in which social justice has not been achieved?

5. What would it take for the "restorative lens" to be a full-blown paradigm?

6. Where do traditional goals of criminal justice such as incapacitation, deterrence, and rehabilitation fit in a restorative model? Do they fit?

7. What about so-called victimless crimes? Do such offenses exist? How should they be dealt with?

8. Are offenses by corporations different than those committed by individuals? How should they be handled?

9. Herman Bianchi has criticized the VORP model for working with individuals in isolation. What should be the role of the families and friends of victims and offenders in a restorative process?

10. What should the role of the community be? How can this role be made concrete? Who is the community anyway?

11. Would we use the term *crime* at all? What if we quit differentiating between "crimes" and other sorts of harms and conflicts? What would be the advantages and disadvantages?

12. How important are the interpersonal dimensions

of crime? Does the author make too much of the attitudes and feelings that victim and offender hold toward one another? Should an effort to address these be a central goal of justice or is this a peripheral issue?

13. What do you make of the author's contention that the victim's needs should be the starting point, but that offender's needs are of equal concern? Is this appropriate? Can it work?

14. The author argues that retributive justice begins with guilt and rights, but that a restorative model begins with needs and obligations. What are the implications of these two starting points?

15. How would the role of "due process" change in a restorative model? What dangers of rights violations might exist? What protections would be needed?

16. A justice model which took victim and offender needs seriously and gave them more participation would result in outcomes which were quite varied. Traditional expectations of uniformity of outcome might be violated. What are the implications of this? How do you see this?

17. Discuss the term *vindication*. What is its biblical meaning? (See, e.g., Psalm 103:6.) What does it mean to you? What might it mean for victims?

18. Given the needs that have been identified here, in what ways can the church assist in the healing of victims and offenders?

19. What about the "dangerous few" in a restorative model? What should be done with them? How should this be decided?

20. Some states are increasing victims' involvement by allowing them input into the sentencing process. What happens when this is done within the existing adversarial, retributive system?

21. The author argues that the present system exaggerates the public dimensions and minimizes the pri-

vate dimensions of crime. What are the public dimensions of crime, and how should they be addressed within a restorative framework?

22. What should be the role of coercion in a restorative model? Should victims be coerced to participate? Should offenders? What are the implications?

23. The present system creates many opportunities for the abuse of power, but a restorative model would leave opportunities as well. Where might these occur? What could be done to minimize them?

24. Think of justice as a communication system, designed to send various messages. What messages does the present system seek to send, and to whom? What messages does it actually send? What messages would a restorative system need to send, and how might it do this?

25. What will society's responsibilities be in a restorative approach, and to whom?

26. What are the meanings of *accountability* in the retributive and the restorative approaches? How important should such accountability be? How can it be implemented?

27. What are some of the necessary rituals in the healing and justice process? When and where should they occur? How could the church be helpful in this?

28. Is there a legitimate role for punishment? If so, in what circumstances and to what end? How can its misuse be minimized?

Activities

1. Ignoring for the moment the questions of how to implement it, try to design an approach to "crime" which is thoroughly restorative. What would it look like?

2. Take a case example. Design a restorative process and outcome for the case. Keep in mind the "four di-

mensions of harm" as well as key elements of the restorative model. When done, test your outcome against the "Restorative Justice Yardstick" in the appendix or develop a yardstick of your own.

Think carefully about where to start. What are the primary needs that must be met? Who can best decide what they are and how they should be met? What are the primary goals and concerns that need to be addressed in your response?

Now look at what normally happens in such a case. (Or, if using an actual case, examine what the actual outcome was.)

Chapter 11
Where from Here?

Questions

1. What is the proper role of the state in the justice process? How would it change in a restorative model?

2. Do either of these models contain inherent cultural, racial, or sexual biases? If so, are these biases inherent in the concept or can they be modified to be less reflective of a white, middle-class, male perspective?

3. How do the retributive and the restorative models look from a feminist perspective? What are their strengths and weaknesses from that perspective? Taking seriously feminists' concerns about power, process, and goals, would anything need to change in the restorative model?

4. What are some of the political and institutional dynamics which might affect possibilities for a shift in our justice paradigm? What are the possibilities for an actual paradigm shift?

5. How can the church practice restorative justice internally? (See, for example, the Mennonite Conciliation Resources in the appendix.)

6. What would happen if we "civilized" the law, treating "criminal" offenses much like other harms and conflicts? What special procedures and safeguards, if any, might be needed?

7. How will you respond differently to crime and other harms or conflicts now that you have read this book?

Activities

1. Starting with the author's discussions of the early-modern and the Japanese systems, imagine and discuss what a "two-track" system might look like in our society today. What would the two systems look like? How would it be decided which track is to be used when?

2. List and discuss some "interim strategies." What goals and programs can be implemented now, under less than ideal circumstances, which nevertheless might take us in the direction of restorative justice?

Select Bibliography

Auerbach, Jerold S.
  1983 *Justice Without Law?* New York: Oxford University Press.

Babcock, William G., ed.
  1987 "The Future of Corrections." *The Prison Journal.* Vol. LXVII, No. 2.

Bard, Morton and Sangrey, Dawn
  1986 *The Crime Victim's Book.* New York: Brunner-Mazel. 2d edition.

Berman, Harold J.
  1975 "The Religious Foundations of Western Law," in *The Catholic University of America Law Review*, Vol. 24, No. 3: 490-508.

  1983 *Law and Revolution: The Formation of the Western Legal Tradition.* Cambridge, Mass.: Harvard University Press.

Bianchi, Herman
  1984 *A Biblical Vision of Justice.* Issue No. 2 of *New Perspectives on Crime and Justice: Occasional Papers.* Akron, Pa.: Mennonite Central Committee.

Bianchi, Herman and Swaaningen, Rene van, eds.
  1986 *Abolitionism: Towards a Non-repressive Approach to Crime.* Amsterdam: Free University Press.

Blad, John R., Hans van Mastrigt, and Niels A. Uildriks, eds.
  1987 *The Criminal Justice System as a Social Problem: An Abolitionist Perspective.* Rotterdam, Netherlands: Erasmus University.

Boecker, Hans Jochen
  1980 *Law and the Administration of Justice in the Old Testament and Ancient East.* Minneapolis: Augsburg Publishing House.

Christie, Nils
  1981 *Limits to Pain.* Oslo, Norway: Universitetsforlaget. Distributed in the U.S. by Columbia University Press.

  1984 *Crime, Pain and Death.* Issue No. 1 of *New Perspectives on Crime and Justice: Occasional Papers.* Akron, Pa.: Mennonite Central Committee.

Cohen, Stanley, ed.
  1986 *Contemporary Crises: Law, Crime and Social Policy.* Vol. 10, No. 1. Dordrecht/Boston/Lancaster: Martinus Nifhoff Publishers. Available from Kluwer Academic Publishers Group, Distribution Center, P. O. Box 322, 3300 AH Dordrecht, Netherlands.

Cohen, Stanley
  1985 *Visions of Social Control.* New York: Basil Blackwell.

Cohen, Stanley and Andrew Scull, eds.
  1983 *Social Control and the State.* New York: St. Martin's Press.

Cullen, Francis T. and Karen E. Gilbert
  1982 *Reaffirming Rehabilitation.* Cincinnati: Anderson Publishing Co.

Currie, Elliott
  1985 *Confronting Crime: An American Dilemma.* New York: Pantheon Books.

Feeley, Malcolm M.
  1979 *The Process Is the Punishment: Handling Cases in a Lower Criminal Court.* New York: Russell Sage Foundation.

  1983 *Court Reform on Trial: Why Simple Solutions Fail.* New York: Basic Books.

Fortune, Marie Marshall
  1983 *Sexual Violence: The Unmentionable.* New York: Pilgrim Press.

Galaway, Burt
  1988 "Restitution as Innovation or Unfulfilled Promise?" Federal Probation, Vol. XII, No. 3: 3-14.

Galaway, Burt and Hudson, Joe, eds.
  1981 *Perspectives on Crime Victims.* St. Louis, Mo.: C. V. Mosby Company.

Gatrell, V. A. C., Lenman, B., and Parker, G., eds.
  1980 *Crime and the Law: A Social History of Crime in Western Europe Since 1500.* London: Europa Publications.

Gaylin, Willard, Ira Glasser, Steven Marcus, and David J. Rothman
  1981 *Doing Good: The Limits of Benevolence.* New York: Pantheon Books.

Griffiths, John
  1970 "Ideology in Criminal Procedure or a Third 'Model' of the Criminal Process." *The Yale Law Journal,* Vol. 79, No. 3, 359-415.

Harris, T. Kay
  1983 "Strategies, Values, and the Emerging Generation of
        Alternatives to Incarceration." *New York University
        Review of Law and Social Change*, Vol. XII, No. 1,
        141-170.

  1987 "Moving into the Millenium: Toward a Feminist Vi-
        sion of Justice." *The Prison Journal.* Vol. LXVII, No.
        2: 27-38.

  1987 "Observations of a 'Friend of the Court' on the Fu-
        ture of Probation and Parole." *Federal Probation*,
        Dec.: 12-21.

Ignatieff, Michael
  1978 *A Just Measure of Pain: The Penitentiary in the Indus-
        trial Revolution, 1750-1850*. New York: Pantheon
        Press.

  1982 "State, Civil Society, and Total Institutions: A Cri-
        tique of Recent Social Histories of Punishment,"
        in *Crime and Justice: An Annual Review of Research*,
        Vol. 3. Michael Tonry and Norval Morris, eds. U.
        of Chicago, pp. 153-192.

Kerans, Patrick
  1982 *Punishment vs. Reconciliation: Retributive Justice and
        Social Justice in the Light of Social Ethics*. Kingston,
        Ont.: Queen's Theological College.

Kuperstock, Kit
  1985 *Worried About Crime? Constructive Approaches to
        Violence*. Scottdale, Pa.: Herald Press.

Lampen, John
  1987 *Mending Hurts*. London, England: Quaker Home
        Service.

Langbein, John H.
  1974 *Prosecuting Crime in the Renaissance, England, Germany
        and France*. Cambridge Mass.: Harvard University
        Press.

Leshan, Lawrence and Margenau, Henry
  1982 *Space and Van Gogh's Sky: Physical Reality and Beyond*.
        New York: Collier Books.

Lind, Millard
  1986 *The Transformation of Justice: From Moses to Jesus*.
        Issue No. 5 of *New Perspective on Crime and Justice:
        Occasional Papers*. Akron, Pa.: Mennonite Central
        Committee.

Lord, Janice Harris
  1988 *No Time for Goodbyes: Coping with Sorrow, Anger and
        Injustice After a Tragic Death*. Ventura, Calif.: Path-
        finder Publishing.

Mackey, Virginia
  1981 *Punishment in the Scriptures and Traditional Judaism:
        Christianity and Islam*, a published paper present-
        ed to the National Religious Leaders Consultation
        on Criminal Justice; Convened by the National
        Council on Crime and Delinquency in Claremont,
        Calif.

MacCullum-Paterson, Morton
  1988 *Towards a Justice That Heals*. Toronto, Canada: The
        United Church Publishing House.

Magee, Doug
  1983 *What Murder Leaves Behind: The Victim's Family*. New
        York: Dodd, Mead and Company.

Marshall, Tony F.
  1985 *Alternatives to Criminal Courts: The Potential for Non-
        judicial Dispute Settlement*. Brookfield, Vt.: Gower
        Publishing Co.

Matthews, Roger, ed.
1988 *Informal Justice?* London: Sage Publications.

McHugh, Gerald Austin
1978 *Christian Faith and Criminal Justice: Toward a Christian Response to Crime and Punishment.* New York: Paulist Press.

Neiderbach, Shelley
1986 *Invisible Wounds: Crime Victims Speak.* New York: The Hayworth Press.

Neufeld, Tom Yoder
1982 *Guilt and Humanness: The Significance of Guilt for the Humanization of the Judicial-Correctional System.* Kingston, Ont.: Queen's Theological College.

Patrick, Dale
1985 *Old Testament Law.* Atlanta: John Knox Press.

Pendleton, John
1987 *More Justice, Less Law.* Issue No. 6 of *New Perspectives on Crime and Justice: Occasional Papers.* Akron, Pa.: Mennonite Central Committee.

Pepinsky, Harold E.
1976 *Crime and Conflict: A Study of Law and Society.* New York: Academic Press.

Reiman, Jeffrey H.
1979 *The Rich Get Richer and the Poor Get Prison: Ideology, Class and Criminal Justice.* New York: John Wiley and Sons.

Rothman, David J.
1971 *The Discovery of Asylum: Social Order and Disorder in the New Republic.* Boston: Little, Brown and Co.

1980 *Conscience and Convenience: The Asylum and Its Alternatives in Progressive America.* Boston: Little, Brown and Co.

Schafer, Stephen
1968 *The Victim and His Criminal.* New York: Random House.

Scheingold, Stuart A.
1984 *The Politics of Law and Order: Street Crime and Public Policy.* New York: Longman.

Smedes, Lewis B.
1984 *Forgive and Forget: Healing the Hurts We Don't Deserve.* New York: Pocket Books.

Spierenburg, Pieter
1984 *The Spectacle of Suffering: Executions and the Evolution of Repression.* Cambridge, England: Cambridge University Press.

Stein, Vivien
1987 *Bricks of Shame: Britain's Prisons.* New York: Viking Penguin.

Stephens, Gene
1986 "Participatory Justice: The Politics of the Future." *Justice Quarterly.* Vol. 3, No. 1:67-82.

Sullivan, D.
1980 *The Mask of Love: Corrections in America—Toward a Mutual Aid Alternative.* Port Washington, N.Y.: Kennikatk Press.

Swartley, Willard M., ed.
1982 *The Bible and Law.* Occasional Papers No. 3 of the Council of Mennonite Seminaries. Elkhart, Ind.: Institute of Mennonite Studies.

Umbreit, Mark
1985 *Crime and Reconciliation: Creative Options for Victims and Offenders.* Nashville: Abingdon Press.

Van Ness, Dan
  1986 *Crime and Its Victims.* Downers Grove, Ill.: Inter-
        varsity Press.

Van Ness, Dan, Zehr, Howard and Harris, T. Kay
  1989 *Justice: The Restorative Vision.* Issue No. 7 of *New
        Perspectives on Crime and Justice: Occasional Papers.*
        Akron, Pa.: Mennonite Central Committee.

Weisser, Michael R.
  1979 *Crime and Punishment in Early Modern Europe.* Atlan-
        tic Highlands, N.J.: Humanities Press.

Wright, Martin
  1982 *Making Good: Prisons, Punishment and Beyond.*
        London: Burnett Books Ltd.

  1988 "From Retribution to Restoration: A New Model for
        Criminal Justice." *New Life: The Prison Service
        Chaplaincy Review.* Vol. 5: 42-49.

Wright, Martin and Galaway, Burt, eds.
  1989 *Mediation and Criminal Justice: Victims, Offenders and
        Community.* London: Sage Publications.

Yoder, Perry, B.
  1987 *Shalom: The Bible's Word for Salvation, Justice and
        Peace.* Newton, Kans.: Faith and Life Press.

Zehr, Howard
  1985 *Retributive Justice, Restorative Justice.* Issue No. 4 of
        *New Perspectives on Crime and Justice: Occasional
        Papers.* Akron, Pa.: Mennonite Central Committee.

Zehr, Howard and Sears, Earl
  1982 *Mediating the Victim-Offender Conflict.* Akron, Pa.:
        Mennonite Central Committee.

Sources of Additional Information

Office of Criminal Justice
Mennonite Central Committee U.S.
107 W. Lexington Ave.
Elkhart, IN 46516
U.S.A.
Resources on VORP and other issues.
  List and newsletter available.

Victim Offender Ministries Program
Mennonite Central Committee Canada
50 Kent Ave.
Kitchener, ON N2G 3R1
Canada
Resources on VORP and other issues.
  List and newsletter available.

U.S. Association for Victim-Offender Mediation
PACT Institute of Justice
254 South Morgan Blvd.
Valparaiso, IN 46383
U.S.A.
Resources on VORP. List and newsletter available.

Mennonite Conciliation Service
Mennonite Central Committee
Box M
Akron, PA 17501
U.S.A.
Resources and training on mediation. Newsletter available.

Forum for Initiatives in Reparation and Mediation (FIRM)
19 London End
Beaconsfield
Bucks HP9 2HN
England
Resources on mediation and reparation. Newsletter available.

Presbyterian Criminal Justice Program
100 Witherspoon St.
Louisville, KY 40202
U.S.A.
Resources on criminal justice issues.

Justice Fellowship
P.O. Box 17181
Washington, DC 20041-0181
U.S.A.
Programmatic and legislative services. Newsletter available.

The Christian Peace Shelf

The Christian Peace Shelf is a selection of Herald Press books and pamphlets devoted to the promotion of Christian peace principles and their applications. The editor (appointed by the Mennonite Central Committee Peace Section) and an inter-Mennonite board represent the historic concern for peace within these constituencies.

For Serious Study

Aukerman, Dale. *Darkening Valley* (1989). An analysis of nuclear war from a biblical perspective calling for all-out resistance to the idolatry of militarism.

Durland, William R. *No King but Caesar?* (1975). A Catholic lawyer looks at Christian violence.

Enz, Jacob J. *The Christian and Warfare* (1972). The roots of pacifism in the Old Testament.

Friesen, Duane K. *Christian Peacemaking and International Conflict* (1986). Realistic pacifism in the context of international conflict.

Hershberger, Guy F. *War, Peace, and Nonresistance* (third edition, 1969). A classic comprehensive work on nonresistance in faith and history.

Hornus, Jean-Michel. *It Is Not Lawful for Me to Fight* (1980). Early Christian attitudes toward war, violence, and the state.

Kaufman, Donald D. *What Belongs to Caesar?* (1969). Basic arguments against voluntary payment of war taxes.

Keim, Al, and Grant Stoltzfus. *Politics of Conscience* (1988). Traces the efforts of the historic peace churches to gain alternative service for conscientious objectors, 1917-1955.

Lassere, Jean. *War and the Gospel* (1962). An analysis of Scriptures related to the ethical problem of war.

Lind, Millard C. *Yahweh Is a Warrior* (1980). The theology of warfare in ancient Israel.

Ramseyer, Robert L. *Mission and the Peace Witness* (1979). Implications of the biblical peace testimony for the evangelizing mission of the church.

Trocmé, André. *Jesus and the Nonviolent Revolution* (1975). The social and political implications of the year of Jubilee in the teachings of Jesus.

Yoder, John H. *The Original Revolution* (1972). Essays on Christian pacifism.

_____. *Nevertheless* (1971). The varieties and shortcomings of religious pacifism.

Zehr, Howard J. *Changing Lenses* (1990). Experiential, historical, and biblical paradigms for understanding crime and justice.

For Easy Reading

Beachey, Duane. *Faith in a Nuclear Age* (1983). A Christian response to war.

Drescher, John M. *Why I Am a Conscientious Objector* (1982). A personal summary of basic issues for every Christian facing military involvements.

Eller, Vernard. *War and Peace from Genesis to Revelation* (1981). Explores peace as a consistent theme developing throughout the Old and New Testaments.

Kaufman, Donald D. *The Tax Dilemma: Praying for Peace, Paying for War* (1978). Biblical, historical, and practical considerations on the war tax issue.

Kraybill, Donald B. *Facing Nuclear War* (1982). Relates Christian faith to the chief moral issue of our time.

_____. *The Upside-Down Kingdom* (1990). A fresh study of the synoptic Gospels on affluence, warmaking, status-seeking, and religious exclusivism.

McSorley, Richard. *New Testament Basis of Peacemaking* (1985). A Jesuit makes the case for biblical pacifism.

Miller, John W. *The Christian Way* (1969). A guide to the Christian life based on the Sermon on the Mount.

Sider, Ronald J. *Christ and Violence* (1979). A sweeping reappraisal of the church's teaching on violence.

Steiner, Susan Clemmer. *Joining the Army That Sheds No Blood* (1982). The case for biblical pacifism written for teens.

Stoner, John K. and Lois Barrett. *Letters to American Christians* (1989). Pithy essays about who Jesus really is and what his salvation has to do with the nuclear arms race.

Wenger, J. C. *The Way of Peace* (1977). A brief treatment on Christ's teachings and the way of peace through the centuries.

Yoder, John H. *He Came Preaching Peace* (1985). Bible lectures addressed to persons already involved in the Christian peace movement.

_____. *What Would You Do?* (1983). A serious answer to a standard question.

For Children

Bauman, Elizabeth Hershberger. *Coals of Fire* (1954). Stories of people who returned good for evil.

Eitzen, Ruth. *The White Feather* (1987). Based on the experience of a Quaker family who treated the Indians as friends and equals.

Lenski, Lois, and Clyde Robert Bulla. *Sing for Peace* (1985). Simple hymns on the theme of living with others.

Minshull, Evelyn. *The Cornhusk Doll* (1987). Tells how the gift of a cornhusk doll in a pioneer setting brought peace and friendship where there had been hatred and mistrust.

Moore, Joy Hofacker. *Ted Studebaker: A Man Who Loved Peace* (1987). A picture storybook of a conscientious objector who was killed in Vietnam while serving as a volunteer agriculturist.

Smucker, Barbara Claassen. *Henry's Red Sea* (1955). The dramatic escape of 1,000 Russian Mennonites from Berlin following World War II.

The Author

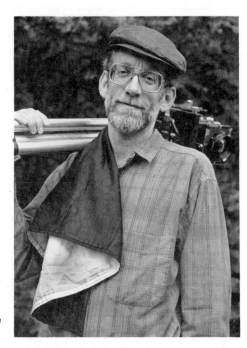

Howard Zehr is a writer and consultant on criminal justice issues. Since 1979, he has served as director of the Mennonite Central Committee U.S. Office of Criminal Justice. He was instrumental in developing the first Victim Offender Reconciliation Program (VORP) in the U.S. and has helped many other communities start similar programs. Zehr has frequently served as speaker and consultant on criminal justice issues in the U.S., Canada, and the United Kingdom. He has authored numerous articles, booklets, and handbooks.

After graduating from Morehouse College in Atlanta, Georgia, Zehr received an M.A. from the University of Chicago and a Ph.D. in European history from Rutgers University with a specialty in social history. His 1976 book, *Crime and the Development of Modern Society,* is an important work in the history of crime.

Prior to assuming his work with VORP and Mennonite Central Committee, Zehr was associate professor of humanities and history at Talladega College, Talladega, Alabama.

He and his wife, Ruby Friesen Zehr, formerly of Manitoba, Canada, are members of the Southside Fellowship in Elkhart, Indiana. They have two teenage daughters, Nicole and Kori.